A Myopic Life Resonated Brink of the *Abyss*

A MYOPIC LIFE RESONATED FROM THE BRINK OF THE *Abyss*

SIMEON W. JOHNSON

PRIMIX
PUBLISHING
THE WRITE CHOICE

Primix Publishing
11620 Wilshire Blvd
Suite 900, West Wilshire Center, Los Angeles, CA, 90025
www.primixpublishing.com
Phone: 1 (888) 585-7476

© 2021 Simeon W. Johnson. All rights reserved.

No part of this book may be reproduced, stored in a retrieval system, or transmitted by any means without the written permission of the author.

Published by Primix Publishing   04/21/2021

ISBN: 978-1-955177-06-1(sc)
ISBN: 978-1-955177-07-8(e)

Library of Congress Control Number: 2021907973

Any people depicted in stock imagery provided by iStock are models, and such images are being used for illustrative purposes only.

Certain stock imagery © iStock.

Because of the dynamic nature of the Internet, any web addresses or links contained in this book may have changed since publication and may no longer be valid. The views expressed in this work are solely those of the author and do not necessarily reflect the views of the publisher, and the publisher hereby disclaims any responsibility for them.

Contents

Chapter 1.	Early Childhood Experience	1
Chapter 2.	An Awesome, Miraculous Act of Salvation from the Brink of the Abyss to a Changed Life	11
Chapter 3.	God's Promise Is Still Available to Us	16
Chapter 4.	Writing of God's Own Hand	21
Chapter 5.	God Works in Mysterious Ways	38
Chapter 6.	What Is a Testimony?	51
Chapter 7.	Short Biography	56
Chapter 8.	Faith in Action	60
Chapter 9.	Final Appeal	69
Chapter 10.	The Perfect Blood Transfusion That Is Safe	77

Introduction

Myopic Life Resonated from the Brink of the Abyss is a true story extraordinaire, which I am privileged to share my story through written words, emphasizing that words are the tools of thoughts by which men and women do most of their thinking and communicate with each other. It broadens horizon, increase overall knowledge, and infuse your conversation with authenticity!

Most aspiring authors dream to have their name nominated into the pantheon of American literature. The most important thing, however, is to have your name, and mine, written indelibly in the Book of Life, which is far better!

1

Early Childhood Experience

Before I begin my testimony of the awesome experience I've had with the Lord, permit me to segue into the subject matter with a brief synopsis of my childhood experiences and family history.

My name is Simeon Johnson.

Born in the district of Swabys Hope, Parish of Manchester, Jamaica, West Indies. I am the youngest son of a family of ten brothers and three sisters. Immigrated to Toronto, Canada, in 1966, I came to the USA in 1967. Today I am a loyal citizen of the United States of America.

I am what you would call a selfmotivated person who loves God and country. I am also a goaloriented per- son. I like to set goals that are realistically attainable.

Some people set goals that severely limit their poten- tial. Others set goals that are unrealistic. As a selfmoti- vated person, I initiate the first step to broaden my hori- zon and to increase my overall knowledge. I am an avid reader with an insatiable thirst for knowledge, not as an egotist, however, but an altruist.

Previous occupation: radio/television electronics technician, welder, shipbuilder, and housing inspector

Hobbies: reading, electronics, book clubs, and sports However admirable these goals and interests may be, I have a more honorable goal in mind: to run this race with patience, looking unto Jesus, the author and finisher of my faith.

After the passing of my dear mother when I was just an infant, I was raised by the youngest of my three sisters, my father, and a few of my older brothers, who were still living at home with us at that time. I can vividly remem- ber a few memorable experiences of my early childhood— one being a severe laceration I sustained over my right eye, the scar of which I visibly bear even to this day.

I remember bleeding profusely, then my mother picked me up tenderly in her arms, cleaned me up, and gave me a bottle of baby tea to pacify me. I also remember my mother rocking me on her knee before putting me to bed at night, after telling me bedtime stories (a childhood experience every child is nurtured by).

One very sad experience I remember, however, was when my mother suffered a severe laceration on her leg. There was lots of blood gushing from her wound. The horrendous sight of blood gave my tenuous heart a very frantic experience of fright and poignant shock—an expe- rience that can only be described as a very special mother and child maternal bond, one that will never be broken as long as I live.

Also, I remember my mother being very sick and not able to get adequate medical care because in those days living in the rural area of Jamaica, West Indies, and being poor, a doctor's care with adequate medical treat- ment was a luxury my family could not afford.

The next thing I remember about my mother: this poor young boy, early in his childhood, before he even began kindergarten school, watched his mother suffer a fatal heart attack. She fell from her sick bed onto the floor between the chairs, gasping for the breath of life. It was a very horrifying experience. It terrifies me every time I think about it.

As a young child, I stood there—not knowing what to do. I commiserated helplessly as I witnessed my moth- er's demise and couldn't do anything to alleviate her suf- fering. I watched in solicitous horror, not knowing what to do. I ran and called my father from the field. By the time my father got to her, it was too late; my mother had passed away.

When I started kindergarten school, I had a pen-chant for friends. I was plagued with the onerous label of being a motherless child throughout kindergarten and grade school. The label had a negative approbation on my life. Life denied me at a very early age of what a mother's love is really like. For those of you who have been raised by a loving mother, from cradle to adulthood, you are now the expert on this very sensitive subject. I can only concur.

At this time, I would like to tell you of an incident that occurred early in my childhood during grade school.

God, however, may not sanction this incident, but let God be the judge of that (Gen. 31:24).

My story is similar to Jacob's deception of his fatherinlaw, by the speckling and spotting of his fatherin-law's cattle found in Genesis 30:33–43 and 31:24.

Jacob, the supplanter, as the name implies (Gen. 27:36), exerted trickery to receive compensation for his wages. As it is written, however, "Who God blesses, no man can curse" (Gen. 31:24, Deut. 23:4–5).

If the Lord can forgive Jacob and many others of such duplicity, including myself, so will he forgive you and all who will ask for his mercy and forgiveness!

One day, while I was in grade school in Jamaica, West Indies, there was this young boy who was accused of stealing five shillings from his teacher's pocketbook. Five shillings, however, were part of the British currency at that time.

The incident had a large group of us youngsters, including the teacher, searching all around the parame-ters of the school ground for the money. While the boy was being accused, and ultimately flogged, I spotted the money on the ground—put my foot on top of it, cleverly picked it up, and put it in my pocket.

Now you and I know that that was a cunning thing to do! However, the Lord has forgiven me of that sin, as he has forgiven Jacob and others. Again, please read Genesis 31:11–13 and verse 24.

What did I do with that money is the question you may be asking.

Well it will come as a big surprise to many that I did not use it to buy candy, cookies, marbles, or comic books! I took it home. Without telling anyone, I went and bought the first King James Bible I have ever owned. And remember, I was just a young boy in the fifth or sixth grade at that time. I did not know Christ as my Savior until I was seventeen years old.

I do believe, however, that by reading that Holy Bible, an early seed of faith was planted in my heart, which led to my conversion later on in my life.

With all that said, when I think of my childhood and what the Lord has saved me from—how Christ took upon himself my sins and the sins of the world, including the flogging, scourging, and shame and reproach of all the world—I am forever grateful!

With these thoughts in mind, I feel like the writer who said, "Must Jesus bear the cross alone, and all the world go free?" Even though we may feel at times like flogging ourselves for the past and present sins in our lives, may we all be reminded that Christ already paid the price for our sins, and physical selfflagellation is not an acceptable form of worship unto God.

Therefore, forgetting those things that are behind and reaching forth unto those things that are before, I press toward the mark for the prize of the high calling of God in Christ Jesus (Phil. 3:13–14).

My father, who was a deacon in a Presbyterian church, had taught us the fear of God by having prayer meetings in our home every Sunday morning. He cus- tomarily sang hymns and read the Bible to us, then con- cluded with prayer.

Because of the early childhood exposure to God, I was brought up with very strict discipline and reverence for God, much different from many of the other kids in our neighborhood.

As a young child, being brought up in a home that taught us the fear of God and to know the difference between good and evil, I always had some fear and rever- ence for God. My father never allowed me to stay out late at night without his permission, only at Christmastime or special occasions.

Being a young boy under a lot of peer pressure see- ing my friends enjoying themselves, by being able to stay out late at night if they wanted to, I would sometimes sneak out with them and stay out a little late until about 10:00 p.m. or so, only to have my back scarred from the flogging that I would receive during the night.

As a teenager, having the rebellious nature that exists among young teens, I made a vow that when I grew a little older and was on my own, I would stay out as late as I wanted to and have all the fun I wanted to have. Is not this the typical characteristic of most teenagers?

My neophyte intellect did not know what plans God had for my life. As I got a little older and graduated from school, I asked my father to help me get an electrical vocational skill, which he refused, and therefore denied me that basic education early in my life.

I finally decided like the prodigal son in the Bible (Luke 16:11–23) to leave home to be on my own.

Unlike the prodigal son, my father did not have any portion of wealth or inheritance to give me. After I left home, I went to Kingston, the capital city of Jamaica, West Indies, at the early age of sixteen.

I worked for pittance wages and endured hardship in the city for about one year. It was during that year while I was in Kingston that I began to experience myriad hard- ship and disillusionment of life. I started to develop cer- tain allergic reactions to various foods and dairy products, which were unknown to me.

It was actually during the formidable years of my childhood where I started to have allergic reactions to var- ious food allergies and caffeine that led to those events in my life, in addition to lactose intolerance, or the inability to digest milk and all kinds of dairy products. The dis- comfort and pain at times were tantamount to labor pain of a woman's travail. Fortunately, the Lord has delivered from those maladies.

Like the woman in the Bible, with the issue of blood, who spent all of her savings, if she had any, and yet she could not be delivered until she met Jesus and touched the hem of his garment (Matt. 9:21). So similar was my situation. All my pittance earnings were depleted on phy- sicians, and none could help me.

God was dealing with my life, but I did not know how to reach out and touch the Lord. I grew somewhat indifferent about God. Sometimes

I wanted to surrender to him, and other times I did not want to have anything to do with Him.

Sometimes I got so frustrated to the point where I thought about committing suicide daily. I remember the times when I went to my bed at night with a knife under my pillow, praying to God to save me, and if my life had gotten too frustrated during the night, I would then slash my throat and end my troubles. I thank God for saving me!

When I woke up the following morning, I was in a state of onerous quandary, yet being thankful to know that I was still alive and had not died in my sins. I was afraid to die and go to hell.

Other times I would find myself working with a sharp machete in my hand. I got so frustrated, raised the machete to my neck, and cried out in despair, ready to slash my throat when something kept saying to me, "Don't do it, or else you will die and go to hell."

I tried the pleasures of sin, but that evanescent dura- tion did not satisfy my soul. God had a purpose for my life. Praise God! I decided to return home. Unlike the prodigal son, I did not have a wealthy father to return home to. Neither was there a fatted calf, a robe, or a ring for my finger awaiting me. But God was waiting there for me.

Having lived in the city, developing manifold taste for city life and a certain amount of independence, I started to explore sin and was able to stay out late at nights. While in the dance hall, I sometimes thought about God and asked myself what if I die in this place? My soul would be lost. I was afraid of dying and going to hell.

The urban life of the city had made me very fashion conscious, obsessed with the lifestyle of glamour, and a desire for the things I was unable to do while under the strict disciplinary control of my father.

Soon I began to hang out with the guys, especially with an old buddy of mine who became one of my best friends. He was preparing me in all the ways of sin, which was becoming more and more desirous to me, every day.

But God had a purpose for my life. His purpose was to rescue me from the stronghold of sin, the path in which I was heading. The broad way that leads to destruction, as the scripture has said. "Enter ye in at the strait gate: for wide is the gate, and broad is the way, that leadeth to destruction, and many there be which go in thereat: Because strait is the gate, and narrow is the way, which leadeth unto life, and few there be that find it" (Matt. 7:13–14). Jesus is Lord and Savior of the world and of all mankind, this truth so lovingly and truthfully declared in the gospel of John.

"For God so loved the world, that he gave his only begotten Son, that whosoever believeth in him should not perish, but have everlasting life. For God sent not his son into the world to condemn the world; but that the world through him might be saved" (John 3:16–17).

How amazing it is that so many people have rejected this awesome personality found only in Jesus, and yet they are so awestruck by the aura of some mere mortals, like movie stars and various worldrenowned personalities.

But, oh how they do not realize that Jesus is the only one who can transform human lives into something more beautiful than the outward appearance that can only last for a little while.

In studying the scripture, we find confirmation of the Word of God that reads in this wise: "But the Lord said unto Samuel, Look not on his countenance, or on the height of his stature; because I have refused him: for the Lord seeth not as man seeth; for man looketh on the outward appearance, but the Lord looketh on the heart" (1 Sam. 16:7).

"The heart is deceitful above all things, and desper- ately wicked: who can know it? I the Lord searches the heart. I try the reins, even to give every man according to his ways, and according to the fruit of his doings" (Jer. 17:9–10).

"For we are but of yesterday, and know nothing, because our days upon earth are a shadow: So are the paths of all that forget God; and the hypocrite's hope shall perish: Whose hope shall be cut off, and whose trust shall be a spider's web" (Job 8:9, 13–14).

But we believers have a better hope, one that tran-scends all other hopes and gleaming personalities in this life.

When we shall see Jesus the Son of God in all his splendid glory, the one who saved us by his grace. His smiling face transcends all races, all cultures, all religions, and all other personalities heaven and earth has ever known.

This same Jesus, who has supernaturally changed my life, can also change your life by giving you a brand new life if you will only let him into your heart today, as he stands at your door knocking, if you hear his voice. Harden not your heart, and let him in; he will save you, cleanse, and make whole.

So far I have given you a brief chronology of my family history and my childhood experience. The focus here is not to talk a whole lot about my family history. Later on in my testimony, I will discuss briefly some of my accomplishments and successes in life, in spite of the many obstacles that stood in my way. However, the main purpose of my testimony is to talk about Jesus Christ, the Son of the living God, and the miracle of salvation He has brought in my life.

Now the time has come for me to explain the most glorious and awesome experience that could ever happen to a sinful mortal man. And that's the miracle of salvation. But before I go into details, let me explain briefly some of the mysterious events that took place in my life prior to that most important event.

It was during the early years of my adolescent life that God began to draw my attention through various frightening dreams that really shook me up.

At times I would dream that the stars were falling from heaven, all around me, yet I was not consumed. I was running to and fro, crying out to God to save me from death and hell. It was like the end of the world; I was not ready to meet God.

Other times, I would dream that it was the end of the world. Judgment day had come, and I was running away from God.

Oh, how I did not realize that there is no hiding place from God. David the Psalmist declares,

> Whither shall I go from thy spirit? Or whither shall I flee from thy presence? If I ascend up into heaven, thou art there; if I make my bed in hell, behold, thou art there. If I take the wings of the morning, and dwell in the uttermost parts of the sea; Even there shall thy hand lead me, and thy right hand shall hold me. If I say,

surely the darkness shall cover me; even the night shall be light about me. Yea, the darkness hideth not from thee; but the night shineth as the day: the darkness and the light are both alike to thee. (Ps. 139:7–12)

When I awoke from my sleep, I was filled with grat- itude that I was still alive, that the world had not come to an end, and that there was still opportunity for me to give my life to Jesus before it was too late. Thank God!

My sister, who raised me from when I was a little child after my mother had passed away, recently got saved in a little Pentecostal church in my district.

She would normally witness to me about Jesus.

I was still living in a state of indifference about God. The devil had such a strong hold on me I could not let loose of sin, even if I wanted to. But a loving and a mer- ciful God had a stronger grip on me than the devil could ever have. Thanks and praise to the Most High God! His name is worthy to be praised! From the rising of the sun to the going down of the same, praised be the name of the Lord.

Oh! One other important thing worth mentioning here! About a confrontation between my natural father, my sister, and the devil over my sister's conversion.

I can vividly recall the night when my sister got saved and decided to make a public confession of her faith in a little Pentecostal church in my district, the pastor of which my father hated with a passion.

That evening, when my sister told my father that she had found the Lord and was going to join the church that night, my father had a fit and got into such a rage that he physically went into the church in the middle of the devo- tion. He walked up and down the aisles of the church, looking for my sister, to drag her out of the church.

But the spirit of the Lord inspired the saints to hide my sister before my father got there. They shouted round and about my father and drove him out of the church.

Thank God for the victory of the battle for my sis- ter's soul. The devil could not snatch her out of God's hand, since the fall of our first parents, Adam and Eve. The ubiquitous presence of sin pervades the hearts and minds of men and women everywhere. The good news is, however, as it is written, "But where sin abounded, grace did much more abound."

Now comes the auspicious moment of truth every- one has been waiting for.

Keep an open mind to what I am about to share with you. After you read, you be the judge. But before you do, ask yourself this question: was it you who died on the cross and washed away my sins, and not only my sins but also the sins of all mankind? Or was it Jesus and Jesus alone, who died on the cross for us all and has all power to forgive sin and to judge the hearts and works of all men?

Please have a pen and paper with you as you read so that you can take note of each scripture that I will direct you to which correlates with each experience the Lord has blessed me with.

Nothing added to or taken away from the Word of God, not one iota! Before I begin, let me pray this prayer of faith, unto my Heavenly Father. The God of all cre- ation! The following is not a pontificate statement, but affirmative.

Dear Jesus, I know that thou art the Christ! The Son of the living God who alone can forgive sins. I know that thou hast heard me when I cried unto you to have mercy upon my soul, and you have blessed in such a way that the doubtful and unbelieving person who will read my testimony will not believe. Therefore, I am asking you, O Lord, to open the eyes of the unbelievers that they may see and know that thou art the true and living God, who alone can do all things according to your good and perfect will, O Lord.

As you have opened the eyes of Elisha's servant, even so, dear Lord Jesus, I pray that you will open the eyes and minds of each reader who wants to believe in you, Dear Lord! Amen. Please read 2 Kings 6:17 and 20.

2

AN AWESOME, MIRACULOUS ACT OF SALVATION FROM THE BRINK OF THE ABYSS TO A CHANGED LIFE

This poor boy! At the early age of seventeen, in the year 1964, it was on a Tuesday afternoon. There I was on my father's bed, taking an afternoon nap, unlike the Apostle Paul's Damascus road conversion (Acts 9:1, 4, 26).

As custom, I always get down on my knees and prayed to God to save my soul before I go to bed at night. My personal Damascus road conversion is this. As

I was going down the road to destruction on my father's bed—not on a procrustean bed having an incubus experi- ence, but a vision from the Lord, with my hands clasped together, looking up toward heaven—I prayed this sim- ple sinner's prayer: "Lord, have mercy upon my soul." Instantly, in the twinkling of an eye, before the last word had left my mouth, *an awesome, miraculous act of salvation took place in my life.* There lying upon my back, looking steadfastly in the face of a holy angel of God with the most glorious of heavenly smiles, with his wings unfolded there standing over me.

It was one of the most perfect and blissful experi- ences any mortal man could ever experience this side of heaven.

Oh, if I had myriad tongues to praise the Lord, I could not adequately praise and exalt the name of the Most High God under whose wings I am securely covered. David the Psalmist, in his exaltation of the Most High, said, "How excellent is thy loving kindness, O God!

Therefore the children of men put their trust under the shadow of thy wings" (Ps. 36:7).

David the Psalmist continued to say, "I will praise thee: for thou hast heard me, and art become my salva- tion" (Ps. 118:21).

In the book of Ruth, we read, "The Lord recom- pense thy work, and a full reward be given thee of the Lord God of Israel, under whose wings thou art come to trust" (Ruth 2:12). Praise God!

Once again, my experience correlates exactly with the Word of God, under whose unfolded wings I have been covered.

The Lord has promised to deliver and will continue to do so. As in Malachi 4:2, the Lord said, "But unto you that fear my name shall the Sun of righteousness arise with healing in his wings; and ye shall go forth, and grow up as calves of the stall."

To all my friends and doubtful Thomases, don't this correlate with the Word of God? Where Jesus said, "I say unto you, that likewise joy shall be in heaven over one sinner that repented, more than over ninety and nine just persons, which need no repentance?" (Luke 15:7).

"Likewise, I say unto you there is joy in the presence of the angels of God over one sinner that repented" (Luke 15:10).

You don't have to believe me, and you may doubt my testimony if you want to, but you cannot deny, nei- ther can you add to nor take away from the infallible word of Jesus, clearly written in Luke 15:7 and 10.

After I was awakened from my sleep, I told my sister of the vision I had. How an angel of the Lord appeared to me in a vision after I prayed the sinner's prayer and asked the Lord to have mercy upon my soul. And how I was going to go to church that Sunday and make a public confession of my faith. She encouraged me to do so.

Like any real convert should, I began my first real act of salvation by seeking after my old friend Junior. I told him what change had taken place in my life, that I was going to church that Sunday, and if he would like to come and join me at the altar. He promised me he would.

I was very excited about having my friend join me at the altar. That Saturday night, I went looking for my friend to confirm his promise to me to go to church with me that Sunday morning, to give his life to Jesus. He reneged on his promise by saying to me that he was not yet ready to make such a commitment. I was very dis- appointed that he wasn't going with me to church that Sunday morning.

I decided if I had to go alone, I would because every man has to give an account for his own sins!

The Bible says, "Work out your own salvation with fear and trembling" (Phil. 2:12). Also let every man be fully persuaded in his own mind. At the Day of Judgment, every knee shall bow, every tongue shall confess.

For it is written, "As I live, saith the Lord, every knee shall bow to me, and every tongue shall confess to God. So then every one of us shall give account of himself to God" (Rom. 14:11–12).

That Sunday morning, I went to the little Pentecostal church in my district. The people were very surprised to see me in church. Because after spending approximately one year in Kingston Town, I was known to be a city lover boy kind of person—not expected to be in a little Pentecostal church on a Sunday morning.

To God be the glory for the great things he has done for me, whereof, I am so thankful to God for my salvation!

That Sunday morning while I was in church, I was so eager to hear the preacher finish his sermon and make his altar call.

As soon as he was finished preaching and the altar call was made, without any hesitation, I walked up to the altar, and there I made a public confession of my faith after I was asked to repeat the sinner's prayer.

Praise God for his redeeming grace and his loving kindness toward me.

Jesus said, "All that the Father giveth me shall come to me; and him that cometh to me I will in no wise cast out" (John 6:37).

My trials and tribulations as a Christian have inten- sified as the devil was publicly humiliated when I publicly confessed Christ as my Savior as a step of my Christian faith.

All of my friends deserted me when they tried unsuccessfully to win me back to their side and failed.

They mocked me and shunned me by telling me that I have made a big mistake, and my Christianity wasn't going to last, but the Lord has helped me to prove them wrong. Thank God!

Not long after I accepted Christ as my personal Savior, I remembered the morning when I got baptized.

It was a custom for the people in the neighborhood to gather around the pool, just to see us get wet by going under cold water.

As my friends and others stood there and watched, I kept my eyes steadfast on Jesus while I was being buried by baptism into death, "even so we also should walk in newness of life" (Rom. 6:4).

The church congregation was singing baptismal songs. A particular song stood out in my memory even to this day. The title of the song was "Goodbye, World, Goodbye, World, Goodbye, World, I Am Gone."

With tears running down my cheeks, I was emo- tionally saying to my friends, "You could have this whole world, but give me Jesus. Having Jesus is all that matters; praise God."

Having been baptized in water, for the remission of my sins, it was soon thereafter I was baptized with the Holy Ghost. I remember the congregation praying with the new converts for this gift. I went outside to the men's room. There I looked up toward heaven and prayed this short prayer, "Lord, help me to receive the Holy Ghost tonight."

I went back inside the church, sat down, and began to pray when suddenly I was in the spirit, on the floor, speaking in other tongues as the spirit gave utterance.

Unfortunately, there are those preachers who preach that the manifestation of God's Holy Spirit doesn't man- ifest itself in today's twentieth or twentyfirst century by faith healing, miracles, and speaking in tongues and other gifts of the Spirit, as the scripture has said. Please read Matthew 10:1, 8; Acts 5:12–16; and Acts 2:4, 39. The Bible speaks of them as "having a form of godliness, but denying the power thereof: from such turn away" (2 Tim. 3:5).

If you should ask them to explain Acts 2, they would tell you that the promise was fulfilled at Pentecost. Therefore it does not apply to us today. They would quote to you Acts 2:38 and stop there. They would not read verse 39, but if you should ask them to explain Acts 2:17–21, they would try to explain it away by saying those scriptures have already been fulfilled.

Dear readers and defenders of the gospel truth, let no man deny you of the promises of God!

The scripture emphatically said, "For the promise is unto you, and to your children, and to all that are far off, even as many as the Lord our God shall call" (Acts 2:39).

You and I today are the offspring and beneficiaries of those promises. Let no one deny you of God's promises.

3

GOD'S PROMISE IS STILL AVAILABLE TO US

In answer to the critics and those who try to limit God's grace and covenant promise to his chosen people that existed at the time of the completion of the gospel, given in Revelation 22:18–21, would it be fair to interpret the writer's warning here in Revelation 22:18–21? It reads as follows:

For I testify unto every man that heareth the words of the prophecy of this book. If any man shall add unto these things, God shall add unto him the plagues that are written in this book. And if any man shall take away from the words of the book of this prophecy, God shall take away his part out of the book of life, and out of the holy city, and from the things which are written in this book. He which testified these things saith, Surely I come quickly. Amen. Even so, come, Lord Jesus. The grace of our Lord Jesus Christ be with you all. Amen.

Nowhere in the completion of the gospel at the end of Revelation 22:18–21 is the inspired writer telling us that the days of miracles—heavenly visitation and the manifestation of the gifts of the Spirit—are over and done away with as some would have you to believe!

The sanction given by the inspired revelator is to guard the sacred canon of the Holy Scripture from pro-fane hands such as those who would like to rewrite certain parts of the scripture to conform to their way of thinking rather than to God's holy way.

To illustrate further why the inspired writer is warn-ing us against adding to or taking away from the Word of God—written and sealed—at the close of the book of Revelation 22:18–21, let us compare scripture with scrip-ture against those that the critics would have us to believe otherwise.

For example, how often have you heard a lay person and those who have claimed to have a monopoly on the interpretation of scriptures quote this well-known verse taken from Exodus 20:5 that reads in this manner, "Thou shalt not bow down thyself to them, nor serve them: for I the Lord thy God am a jealous God, visiting the iniquity of the fathers upon the children unto the third and fourth generation of them that hate me"?

Are we to believe the interpretation of scripture as saying that the visitation of the iniquity of the fathers upon the third and fourth generation of them who hate God are over and applies only to previous generation as quoted above? I don't think so.

Even the harshest critics of presenttime manifesta-tion of God's Holy Spirit, in the form of miracles and other gifts of the Spirit, would agree that the above quota-tion is not just relevant to previous generations.

This applies to today's generation also and to all generations that follow, if the Lord should tarry.

If the application of scripture referring to genera-tion declared by God as given in Exodus 20:5 are relevant today, it's appalling that the critics have so strongly dis-agreed with the interpretation of Joel 2:28–29 and Acts 2:17 and 39 as declared!

"And it shall come to pass afterward, that I will pour out my spirit upon all flesh; and your sons and your daughters shall prophesy, your old men shall dream dreams, your young men shall see visions. And also upon the servants and upon the handmaids in those days will I pour out my spirit" (Joel 2:28–29).

Not only does this apply to previous generations, "but to your children, and to all that are afar off, even as many as the Lord thy God shall call" (Acts 2:39).

God is not dead! He is alive as always. He still speaks to us through his written word and through the Holy Spirit. He may not speak with an audible, sonorous voice. Nevertheless, He is able to manifest Himself to us the- anthropically or otherwise!

Further study of the scripture reveals even more truths and confirmation of promises of the former and latter rain.

Hosea, the prophet, declares, "Then shall we know, if we follow on to know the lord: his going forth is pre- pared as the morning; and he shall come unto us as the rain, as the latter and former rain, unto the earth" (Hosea 6:3).

In comparing scripture with scripture as the Word of God said,

> Study to show thyself approved unto God, a workman that needed not to be ashamed, rightly dividing the word of truth. But shun profane and vain babblings; for they will increase unto more ungodliness. And their word will eat as doth a canker: of whom is Hymenaeus and Philetus; Who concerning the truth have erred, saying that the resurrection is past already; and overthrow the faith of some. Nevertheless the foundation of God standeth sure, having this seal, The Lord knoweth them that are his. (2 Tim. 2:15–19)

By continuing to be guided by the inspired Word of God—taken from Hosea 6:3—we will now turn to Joel 2:23, which reads likewise: "Be glad then, ye children of Zion, and rejoice in the Lord your God: for he hath given you the former rain moderately, and he will cause to come down for you the rain, the former rain, and the latter rain in the first month."

Are there anywhere in these verses of proclaimed promises where the words of God had declared that the former rain and the latter rain has come and past at the day of Pentecost and at the completion of the gospel given in Revelation 22:18–21, as the critics would have you to believe? That the days of miracles and gifts of the Spirit are past and done away at such time as stated above?

No! No! The Word of God has not declared such end of the latter and former rain, neither Hosea 6:3 nor Revelation 22:18–21. Such an end are proclaimed by crit- ics, such as those described in 2 Timothy 2:17–18.

James, the inspired writer long after the day of Pentecost that reads in this wise, also confirms these promises in the New Testament.

"Be patient therefore, brethren, unto the coming of the Lord. Behold, the husbandman waiteth for the precious fruit of the earth, and hath long patience for it, until he receive the early and latter rain. Be ye also patient, establish your hearts: for the coming of the Lord draweth nigh" (James 6:7–8).

Again, the scripture doesn't teach that these prom- ises are no longer available to believers. Only the scoffers are saying this. Their favorite quote when confronted with these truths will be taken from Revelation 22:18–19; they will try to explain it away by saying these signs are no lon- ger working among us. That they were completed during the Pentecostal era and, therefore, cannot be from God. But the truth is Revelation 22:18–19 has not declared unto us that these promises have passed.

He is not saying that for us to easily believe in divine healing and the manifestation of the gifts of the Spirit spo- ken of by the prophets and, most of all, by Christ himself. This is adhered to by us, also declared by the Apostle Paul in 1 Corinthians 12:7–11 about adding to or taking away from the words of the book of this prophecy.

The inspired writer of the book of Revelation is not saying that to us to believe in divine healing and the man- ifestation of the gifts of the spirit as declared above are adding to or taking away from the Word of God!

As we study the word of God and compare scripture with scripture, we have seen that these promises spoken of by Hosea 6:3, Joel 2:23, and Acts 2:17–21 and 39 are not done away with, as the critics would have you to believe. Only when that which is perfect has come will these be done away with, as declared by the apostle Paul who reads in this manner: "For we know in part, and we prophesy in part. But when that which is perfect is come, then that which is in part shall be done away" (1 Cor. 13:9–10).

To the gospel-believing readers armed with these truths, you and I are able to guard against heresy and those who teach contrary doctrine who denies gospel truths.

You and I know the prophetic words of the prophet Amos, which declares,

> Behold, the days come, saith the Lord God, that I will send a famine in the land, not a famine of bread, nor a thirst for water, but of hearing the words of the Lord: And they shall wander from sea to sea, and from the north even to the east, they shall run to and fro to seek the word of the Lord, and shall not find it. In that day shall the fair virgins and young men faint for thirst. They that swear by the sin of Samaria, and say, Thy God, O Dan, liveth; and, The manner of Beersheba liveth; even they shall fall, and never rise up again. (Amos 8:11–14)

These verses quoted in the above paragraph are not to be interpreted as in Revelation 22:18–19.

Again in comparing scripture with scripture, please refer to 1 Corinthians 13:1–13. You, the reader, are to examine the scripture for yourself and find out.

4

WRITING OF GOD'S OWN HAND

As I grew in the fear and knowledge of the Lord, I developed an earnest desire to study and learn many chapters and verses of the Bible, which I've committed to memory, written indelibly upon the tablets of my heart. I also continue to study the Holy Scripture diligently, in prayer and fasting, and supplication before God. The Lord continued to bless me immensely with visions of raptures of his holy presence.

David the Psalmist said, "Blessed is the man that walked not in the counsel of the ungodly, nor standeth in the way of sinners, nor sitteth in the seat of the scornful. But his delight is in the Law of the Lord, and in his law doth he meditate day and night" (Ps. 1:1–2).

My omnifarious readers, it was in a night vision as I was walking down the road to where some of my unsaved friends usually hang out, in a small neighborhood grocery store. The Spirit of the Lord convinced me not to go any farther.

I reasoned in my mind and agreed. That wasn't the place for a Christian to be. Instantly I turned around and started to walk back home when suddenly, in a moment, in the twinkling of an eye, I felt the quickening presence of God's Holy Spirit. I looked up toward heaven, and there in the night vision, appeared unto me the eternal glory of the writing of God's own hand, which read, "ETERNAL GOD AND EVERLASTING FATHER!"

Oh, how I give thanks and praise unto the Most High God. Mortal tongue cannot explain the awesome- ness of the glory of the living God. Being in his presence, just one touch of his glory is enough for mortal man to contain.

It is more than tongue can ever tell. In his presence, you are free from the very consciousness of sin (1 Cor. 15:50–54). Oh, how I give thanks and praise to the Lord God eternal, the everlasting Father!

"How great are his signs! And how mighty are his wonders! His kingdom is an everlasting kingdom, and his dominion is from generation to generation" (Dan. 4:3, 34).

In 2 Corinthians 5:1 we read, "For we know that if our earthly house of this tabernacle were dissolved, we have a building of God, a house not made with hands, eternal in the heavens."

In John 17:1–3, we read, "These words spake Jesus…and said, Father, the hour is come, glorify thy Son, that thy Son also may glorify thee: As thou hast given him power over all flesh, that he should give eternal life to as many as thou hast given him. And this is life eternal, that they might know thee the only true God, and Jesus Christ, whom thou hast sent." Praise God!

Again, we read in Romans 1:20, here Paul is empha- sizing the eternal power and Godhead, "For the invisible things of him from the creation of the world are clearly seen, being understood by the things that are made, even his eternal power and Godhead; so that they are without excuse."

In the book of Daniel, we read of Belshazzar's expe- rience of the mighty hand of God. We read, "In the same hour came forth fingers of a man's hand, and wrote over against the candlestick upon the plaster of the wall of the king's palace: and the king saw the part of the hand that wrote Then the king's countenance was changed, and his thoughts troubled him, so that the joints of his loins were loosed, and his knees smote one against another" (Dan. 5:5–6).

Dear readers, Belshazzar saw the mysterious hand- writing on the wall. He was troubled and was shaking in his shoes because he could not understand the mysterious writing of the hand of God that meant doom for him and his kingdom.

But the *eternal* writing of God's own hand that appeared unto me in the firmament of heaven let me know that God is my *eternal God and everlasting Father*. Praise His holy name!

There are some of you who will not believe me and will pass judgment on my testimony, who will also preach that the days of miracles and heavenly visions are over, and that the Lord is not making heavenly visitations, neither in dreams nor in visions, in these times. This is what the Lord has to say about that in Joel 2:28, "And it shall come to pass afterward, that I will pour out my spirit upon all flesh; and your sons and your daughters shall prophesy, your old men shall dream dreams, your young men shall see visions."

Here is what God continues to say about it in the New Testament, through the apostle Peter in Acts 2:17: "And it shall come to pass in the last days, saith God, I will pour out of my spirit upon all flesh: and your sons and your daughters shall prophesy, and your young men shall see visions, and your old men shall dream dreams."

There you have it, my friends! The infallible Word of God, of which you cannot deny! You may try to explain it away if you can, but even if you search the scripture from Genesis to Revelation, you will not be able to find a scripture that will make null and void the experience that the Lord has blessed me with.

In the book of Isaiah 40:14, "The Lord said, with whom took he counsel, and who instructed him and taught him in the path of judgment, and taught him knowledge, and showed him the way of understanding?" "To whom then will ye liken God? Or what likeness will ye compare unto him?" (Isa. 40:18).

"To whom then will ye liken me, or shall I be equal? Saith the Holy one" (Isa. 40:25).

"Hast thou not known? Hast thou not heard, that the everlasting God, the Lord, the creator of the ends of the earth, fainteth not, neither is weary?" (Isa. 40:28).

In all these scriptures that I have given you, the Word of God has confirmed the *eternal* writing of God that I have seen in my vision from the Lord. Nothing has been added to or taken away from the Word of God.

David the Psalmist also confirmed it when he said, "Lord, thou hast been our dwelling place in all genera- tions. Before the mountains were brought forth, or ever thou hadst formed the earth and the world, even from everlasting to everlasting, thou art God" (Ps. 90:1–2).

Again, the Word of God confirmed the writing of God's holy word, the writing of God that I saw in the night vision in the firmament of heaven that read:

ETERNAL GOD AND EVERLASTING FATHER!

Oh, what awesome splendor is the eternal glory of the Most High God!

To whom will you liken God?

With Him, there is no equal. He is *omnipotent.*

His magnificent, majestic, heavenly bliss is more than tongue can ever tell.

"Now unto the king eternal, immortal, invisible, the only wise God, be honor and glory for ever and ever. Amen" (1 Tim. 1:17).

"But God forbid that I should glory, save in the cross of our Lord Jesus Christ, by whom the world is crucified unto me, and I unto the world" (Gal. 6: 14).

I believe the inerrant Word of God. I also have per- sonally experienced some of his miraculous blessings in my life.

As I continued to grow in the grace and knowledge of the Lord and continued to study the Holy Scripture, in prayer and fasting before the Lord, the Lord continued to bless me spiritually, beyond measure.

Before I continue any further, let me make some- thing very clear here. These experiences that the Lord has blessed me with are not new revelations from the Lord, as some of you might contend, nothing added to or taken away from the words of God that are written in the Bible. All of the experience that the Lord has blessed me with, I have given you the scriptures and will continue to give you the scripture that correlates exactly with what I have said so far.

As it is written in the Bible, it was in the night vision while I was in fellowship with the Lord.

"Now there was a day when the sons of God came to present themselves before the Lord, and Satan came also among them. And the Lord said unto Satan, whence comest thou? Then Satan answered the Lord, and said, From going to and fro in the earth, and from walking up and down in it" (Job 1:6–7).

In this experience, Satan argued with the Lord about my soul. I remember finding myself in God's right hand, while by my other hand; Satan was pulling me away from God. But with the *everlastingly, strong arm of God*, I was delivered from the hand of Satan.

In Deuteronomy 33:27, the Word of God declares, "The eternal God is thy refuge, and underneath are the everlasting arms; and he shall thrust out the enemy from before thee; and shall say, destroy them."

In Psalm 20:6, David declares, "Now know I that the Lord saveth his anointed; he will hear him from his holy heaven with the saving strength of his right hand." You may also read Psalm 44:3 and Luke 1:61.

How can you be sure of the things you've just described, you may ask. The answer is simple! Not pontif- icate, but from the scriptures I've given you.

Dear readers, my testimony is real! My conviction is so strong; the evidence is so overwhelming. It is impos- sible for the visions I have described to you to be of any other power other than that of the *eternal God*!

For these reasons, and like those of the prophets of God, the disciples of Jesus, the reformers, and the heroic men and women of faith—like Luther, a man for his time—John Wycliffe, and all the other loyalists and mis- sionaries who died a martyr's death for Christ with their convictions.

As for my conviction, like most human beings, I would like to live a normal life, free from troubles and cares, persecutions and distress, pain and sufferings, etc. However, when I read of the life and sufferings of all the martyrs who died for the cause of Christ, his holiness, and the righteousness, power, and the glory of the *eternal God*, I am resolved that a martyr's death would be a small price for me to pay, as a token of my love and devotion for Christ.

If you should ask me why do I emphasize the words *eternal God and everlasting Father* so many times in my writing, I will answer with these words.

Because of the Word of God, written by God's own hand in the firmament of heaven, the power and the glory of the awesomeness of God's holy presence that has such an impact on my life, I cannot praise God enough. Therefore, I will continue to lift God up as often as I can. After all, this is the whole purpose of my testimony! And that is to have an impact upon the hearts and minds of all my readers, especially to the unbelievers.

To let them know that God is not dead. The *eternal God* is still alive today and always is!

You may think that my often and frequent reference to the words *eternal God and everlasting Father* is too rep- etitious. This is what the Word of God has to say about giving honor and praises unto the Most High God.

"And the four beasts had each of them six wings… about them; and they were full of eyes within: and rested not day and night, saying, Holy, holy, holy, Lord God Almighty, which was, and is, and is to come. And when those beast give glory and honor and thanks to him that sat on the throne, who liveth for ever and ever, The four and twenty elders fell down before him that sat on the throne, and worshipped him that liveth for ever and ever, and cast their crowns before the throne, saying, Thou art worthy, O Lord, to receive glory and honor and power: for thou hast created all things, and for thy pleasure they are and were created." (Rev. 4:8–11).

Jesus the Crucified Son of God said, "And I, if I be lifted up from the earth, will draw all men unto me" (John 12:32).

In John 3:14–15, Jesus also said, "And as Moses lifted up the serpent in the wilderness, even so must the Son of man be lifted up: That whosoever believeth in him should not perish, but have eternal life."

It is my desire here and always to lift Jesus up—the Son of God who died on the cross, high and lifted up, whither—in our praise and adoration unto the Lord or looking up to Calvary's cross as a point of contact with Jesus our Savior, and be saved.

You may ask me how strong is my conviction, my belief in God, the experiences I have described so far, and what could deter me from my belief?

My belief in God and the manifold experiences he has blessed me with is so strong that I can say beyond the shadow of a doubt and without fear because Jesus said, "And fear not them which kill the body, but are not able to kill the Soul; but rather fear him which is able to destroy both soul and body in hell" (Matt. 10:28, Luke 12:4–5). Therefore I can safely give up my life unto death for Jesus, not by strength nor by might, but by the grace of God.

Nothing that you can do to me can deter me from my faith and my belief in God because the relationship I have with the Lord and the experiences he has blessed me with are real!

Who shall separate us from the love of Christ? Not even if it were possible for me to be placed at the center of ground zero and all the stockpiles of the world nuclear arsenals were to be simultaneously detonated at me.

The most you could do to me is to scatter the ashes and plant the seeds of my faith to the four corners of the earth, wherever men may dwell; therefore, my faith will never die.

There you have it. That's how strong my faith, and conviction, are in the Lord! Praise God.

This is my experience in the night vision from the Lord. This is also a real-life, daily experience in my own life. Now this is what Jesus in the Holy Scripture has to say about this.

Jesus said, "And I give unto them eternal life, and they shall never perish, neither shall any man pluck them out of my hand. My father which gave them me, is greater than all; and no man is able to pluck them out of my Father's hand" (John 10:28–29). Praise God!

"Let God be true but every man a liar" (Rom. 3:4). Oftentimes I would be awakened from my sleep, praising and glorifying God. My Father had thought there was something unusual going on in my life.

The Bible said the natural man cannot understand the Spiritual things of God. "But if our gospel be hid, it is hid to them that are lost." (1 Cor. 4:3). Therefore, the gospel of the kingdom is not esoteric in this context.

Here is what the scripture has to say, "But the nat- ural man received not the things of the Spirit of God: for they are foolishness unto him: neither can he know them, because they are spiritually discerned. But he that is spiri- tual judgeth all things, yet he himself is judged of no man" (1 Cor. 2:14–15).

As I come to the closing chapters of my testimony, of the awesome experiences of dreams and visions from the Lord, there are many other experiences I've had. But I will come to a conclusion with this one, to share with you among the many other memorable ones.

In the early part of my testimony, I've told you about the dreams and visions I've had about judgment and hell, when the angel of the Lord appeared unto me after I prayed the sinner's prayer of salvation and asked the Lord to have mercy upon my soul.

Now this time, the experience is not about running away from the Lord but about being welcomed into the arms of the Most High God, under his wings while the lost sinner was rejected from the presence of the Lord.

It was in the night vision, nothing to compare like the vision John saw in the book of Revelation. However, it was a vision from the Lord, nothing added to or taken away from the Word of God.

"I had a vision of the day of judgment, when all the people, small and great, stood before God" (Rev. 20:12).

There was weeping and wailing and gnashing of teeth. This lady from my hometown, who I personally know, was there standing before God with her child in her arms, weeping before God. Her excuse to the Lord was that her children had kept her from serving God all her life.

My fellow readers, at the Day of Judgment, there will be no excuses. The apostle Paul said, "Ye did run well; who did hinder you that ye should not obey the truth?" (Gal. 5:7).

Dear readers, the Bible said "How shall we escape, if we neglect so great salvation; which at first began to be spoken by the Lord, and was confirmed unto us by them that heard him" (Heb. 2:3).

> For God so loved the world that he gave his only begotten Son, that whosoever believeth in him should not perish, but have everlasting life. For God sent not his Son into the world to condemn the world; but that the world through him might be saved. He that believeth on him is not condemned: but he that believeth not is condemned already, because he hath not believed in the name of the only begotten Son of God. (John 3:16–18)

The apostle Paul said, "For we must all appear before the judgment seat of Christ; that every one may receive the things done in his body, according to the things he hath done, whether it be good or bad. Knowing therefore the terror of the Lord, we persuade men; but we are made manifest unto God; and I trust also are made in your conscience" (2 Cor. 5:10–11).

After I was awakened from my sleep, praising and glorifying God, suddenly my father was awakened by the disturbance, not being able to understand the spiritual things of God.

I told him what had just taken place in my relation- ship with the Lord. His response to me was, "God must truly be dealing with your life."

I was much troubled in my spirit as to how I should approach this dear lady with the exceedingly dreadful news. However, there is still a chance for her to give her heart to Jesus and be saved.

I asked the Lord to give me courage to do so. The Lord did give me courage. I went over to her house and told her of the vision I had of the judgment, how she was among those who were lost by being separated from God. She took the news very somberly.

I went home feeling very relieved. It was like a heavy load had been lifted from my soul.

Let me emphasize this truth here so that there will be no misinterpretation of my statements.

I am not saying that the Lord has given me a mes- sage for this dear lady! I only did what any good Christian should do in that situation, and that is if I see a fellow human being in danger of hell, it is my

Christian duty to warn him or her of the danger of the judgment and hope that the Lord would save their soul.

That is exactly what I did. Not adding anything to or taken away from the Word of God.

During the Christmas season of December 1995, I spoke by phone to my sister in Toronto, Canada. It was during that conversation I learned that this dear lady had given her heart to Jesus some years ago, and is still saved. Praise God for that good news of salvation.

Except for an old buddy, who I have told you about in my previous statements, my sister, and a few other peo- ple—not more than about a half a dozen—I have not told my visions to many people because I do not want to focus any attention to myself. To God be the glory for the great things he has done for me.

I was seventeen years old during the first year of my salvation, when all those wonderful things happened to me.

I often pondered in my heart why God chose to bless me in the manner in which I have been blessed. And why didn't the angel of the Lord reveal his name to me until I read in the Bible about all the people of God who angels of God had appeared to.

In the book of Judges, we read, "Then the woman came and told her husband, saying, a man of God came unto me, and his countenance was like the countenance of an angel of God, very terrible; but I asked him not whence he was, neither told he me his name" (Judg. 13:6). "And Mano h' said unto the angel of the Lord, what

is thy name, that when thy sayings come to pass we may do thee honor? And the angel of Lord said unto him, why asks thou thus after my name, seeing it is a secret?" (Judg. 13:17–18).

There you have it: the absolute proof. All the visions that I have told you corroborated exactly with the scrip- ture. I've not added to or taken away from the word of God.

Unfortunately, there will still be some—in spite of the overwhelming proof of the scripture I've given you— who will still doubt. But so were doubtful Thomas and the scribes and Pharisees who doubted Jesus.

Let me use this analogy here. Case in point, let's say you, the reader, is on a very hot sunny day when there is no cloud in the sky. The sky is bright and clear, and the sun is at its hottest position in the sky. You went out- side, and for a brief moment, you took a quick glance and looked up at the sun. It was amazingly hot and bright. You quickly withdrew your eyes from looking at the sun. You looked around at someone standing nearby. If you should say to that person, "Do you know I've just experienced the brightness of the sun, and I am so amazed at the goodness of God the Creator! How he has placed the sun up in the sky at just the right position so that we are not all con- sumed by its brightness and very hot temperature!"

Suppose that person was to respond to you with these words, "Man, what are you talking about? There is no sun up in the sky!" No one can succumb to that kind of experience you just described.

What would be your response to that person? I am quite sure you would defend, with every aspect and phase of your faith, the experience you've just had.

The point I am trying to make here is this: If the sun, which shines so brightly in the sky, is so overwhelm- ingly convincing and yet there are still those who will not respect its awesome power and accept the Creator, who directs its power, neither should I be surprised if some will not be convinced of my testimony.

In this analogy, it is understood that the phenome- non of the physical sun can scientifically be explained, but who can possibly explain the magnificent splendor of the holiness and glory of the Most High God of whom my soul has been so humbly blessed!

I used the analogy of the physical sun because the evidence is so overwhelming, and I have seen with my own eyes and heard with my own ears "a young man who looked up at the sun and cursed its existence with such irreverent and ungodly disdain."

Psalm 14:1 reads, "The fool hath said in his heart, there is no God."

There are those who say that visions and dreams of today are not from God. But if you are like the skeptic of the character described in this analogy, I do not have to prove anything more to you other than the infallible Word of God in all the scripture I have so far referred you to. But let me say this: It is impossible for my experiences, of visions from the Lord that I've described to you with scripture that corroborated with my claims, to be from any other power than that of the *eternal God*!

No ands, ifs, and buts about it, *period*!

As a matter of fact, I welcome your criticism! I will wear it as a crown of righteousness, which the Lord, the righteous judge, shall give me at that day, as it is written. "Henceforth there is laid up for me a crown of righteous- ness, which the Lord, the righteous judge shall give me at that day: and not to me only, but unto all them that love his appearing" (2 Tim. 4:8).

In 2 Corinthians 4:8, 9, 16–17, the apostle Paul reminds us, "We are troubled on every side, yet not dis- tressed; we are perplexed, but not in despair; Persecuted, but not forsaken; cast down, but not destroyed; for which cause we faint not; but though our outward man perish, yet the inward man is renewed day by day. For our light affliction, which is for a moment, worked for us a far more exceeding and eternal weight of glory."

You may also read 2 Corinthians 6:4–10.

Jesus said, "Blessed are ye, when men shall revile you, and persecute you, and shall say all manner of evil against you falsely, for my sake. Rejoice, and be exceedingly glad; for great is your reward in heaven; for so persecuted they the prophets which were before you" (Matt. 5:11–12).

Jesus the Christ, the Son of God who healed the sick and raised the dead, performed many miracles. He, who was perfect in all his ways, had not committed any sin, was crucified on the cross, died, and rose again on the third day as he said he would (John 2:19–22; Matt. 12:40).

Yet there are those who do not believe him. Neither will they believe me, being a dry tree, compared to Jesus, being the green tree.

Jesus said, "For if they do those things in a green tree, what shall be done in the dry?" (Luke 23:31).

"But the God of all grace, who hath called us unto his eternal glory by Christ Jesus, after that he hath suf- fered a while, makes you perfect, establish, strengthen, settle you. To him be glory and dominion forever and ever. Amen." (1 Pet. 6:10–11).

I was seventeen years old when the Lord gave me these tremendous blessings. Since then, I've ruminated over these blessed events in my life, concerning God's plan for me, what my calling is, and his will for my life. However, I cannot recall, even for one moment, ever questioning the validity of the awesomeness of the omnipotent power of the eternal God.

The quickening of his holy presence of which I have so humbly felt is the evidence of the writing of God's own hand in the firmament of this side of heaven.

Of such power and glory, there is no equal, known or unknown to man. To whom then will ye liken God? Or what likeness, will ye compare unto him?

"To whom then will ye liken me, or shall I be equal? saith the Holy One" (Isa. 40:25).

Therefore, for those of you who may be thinking of interjecting the devil into this equation, relinquish that thought.

"Such thought can only lead to sin. The evidence of truth is overwhelming. For whatsoever is not of faith is sin" (Rom. 14:23).

In the Bible, we read, "Then was brought unto him one possessed with a devil, blind, and dumb: and he healed him, in so much that the blind and dumb both spake and saw" (Matt. 12:22).

> But when the Pharisees heard it, they said, This fellow doth not cast out devils, but by Beelzebub the prince of the devils. And Jesus knew their thoughts, and said unto them, Every kingdom divided against itself is brought to desolation: and every city or house divided against itself shall not stand: And if Satan cast out Satan, he is divided against himself; how shall then his kingdom stand?" (Matt. 12:24–26)

He that is not with me is against me; and he that gathered not with me scattered abroad. (Matt. 12:30)

My friend, I do not have to defend the evidence of truth of which I have so truthfully demonstrated to my readers.

I have kept these things personal to myself all these years, thinking that these are just personal blessings God has blessed me with.

There are those who contend that because since the Holy Scripture has already been written, there are no new messages given to twentiethcentury man. However, I am fully aware of what the scripture has to say about the written Word of God. Therefore, I have nothing to fear or to lose but a lot to gain. "For I am not ashamed of the Gospel of Christ, for it is the power of God unto salva- tion: to the Jew first, and also to the Greek" (Rom. 1:16). I have been very careful in my writing so as not to make any claims where I have not given you the scrip- ture that corroborated with my experience with the Lord. Joel 2:28–32 declares it! Acts 2:17–21 and 39 confirms it. There you have it, the indisputable fact. The infallible Word of God. In 2 Corinthians 13:8, we read, "For we can do nothing against the truth, but for the truth." Dear readers, have you not read it in the scripture?

In Acts 5:29, we read, "Then Peter and the other apostles answered and said, we ought to obey God rather than men."

Verse 32 said, "And we are his witnesses of these things; and so is also the Holy Ghost, whom God hath given to them that obey him."

> Then stood there up one in the council…and said unto them, Ye men of Israel, take heed to yourselves what ye intend to do as touching these men. For before these days rose up Theudas, boasting himself to be somebody. After this man rose up Judas of Galilee in the days of the taxing, and drew away much people after him… And I say unto you, refrain from these men, and let them alone; for if this counsel or this work be of men, it will come to nought. But if it be of God, ye cannot overthrow it; lest haply ye be found even to fight against God. (Acts 5:34–39)

I do recommend that you carefully study these verses for yourself.

One of the reasons why I am coming out this time with this public declaration of my testimony, in written words, is that I have heard some preachers and individuals making a mockery of those people who have claimed to have had dreams and visions from the Lord.

They said that such individuals must have eaten some bad food, took pills, had some illusive dreams, etc.

But oh, my friend, I am not here to defend any other individual's claim. I can only give an account for my own experience with the true and living God.

I have given you my testimony. I have also given you all the scripture that corroborated my claims. There you have all the facts. Try the Spirit and see if it is of God!

Now in reference to the word *illusion*, I dare say this with all due respect to all the linguists and lexicographers who gave us the etymology of the origins of words. There is no word in the human vocabulary that can make null and void the awesome, unspeakable experience that the Lord has blessed me with despite my neophyte, callow experience thirty-five years ago! There are no ands, ifs, and buts about its validity.

Joseph's, Peter's, and Paul's dreams and visions weren't illusions! Neither is mine (Gen. 37:6, Acts 11:5– 18; 1 Cor. 12:1–10).

Of all the people mentioned in the Bible who had dreams and visions from the Lord, if their dreams and visions weren't an illusory experience, neither is mine.

My God is not dead! He is very much alive in this era, as he was in the Bible days.

My own life experience with the Lord demonstrates that fact. "The heavens declare the glory of God; and the firmament sheweth his handiwork. Day unto day uttered speech, and night unto night sheweth knowledge. There is no speech nor language, where their voice is not heard" (Ps. 19:1–3).

If I did not have the proof and the word of God to corroborate with my testimony, I would be commit- ting the unpardonable sin! Therefore, let God be true and every man a liar (Rom. 3:3–4).

Again, let me elaborate on what has been said by those who have made a mockery of heavenly visitation to individuals in this day and age. Again, I can only testify of my own experience with the Lord, because every man has to work out his own salvation with fear and trembling (Phil. 2:12).

Jesus said, "But I say unto you, that every idle word that men shall speak, they shall give account thereof in the Day of Judgment. For by thy words thou salt be jus- tified, and by thy words thou salt be condemned" (Matt. 12:36–37).

The Lord is my witness, and the Word of God is my strength; therefore, I have nothing to fear. For this reason, I therefore challenge, not by strength nor by might, but by faith in the living God Almighty. "For by grace are we saved, through faith; and that not of yourselves: it is the gift of God: Not of works, lest any man should boast" (Eph. 2:8–9).

I dare challenge all the learned minds of this world, whither of the present or in the future. All of the world's most renowned pharmacists, herbalist, clinical psychoan- alysts, etc.

They will not be able to manufacture or produce a formula so potent as to compare to the power and glori- ous transformation of the presence of the Most High God and his holy angels. Such incommunicable, indescribable experience is beyond human power to tell or describe.

And so, my omnifarious readers and those of the household of faith, try the Spirit and see if it is of God from all the scripture given to you so far.

For those of you who would like to refute the evi- dence of the scripture and that of my testimony, like Elijah's challenge to all the false prophets of Baal upon Mount Carmel (1 Kings 18:19–39), in the name of the Lord, I accept the challenge of any man on this earth to a contest of faith. If they can concoct a formula of drugs or pills to induce an illusion of such magnitude and awe- some splendor, like that of the presence of the Most High God, the *eternal God and everlasting Father.*

Oh, blessed be the holy name of our Lord God and Savior Jesus Christ! Isaiah 9:6 declares, "For unto us a child is born, unto us a Son is given; and the government shall be upon his shoulder; and his name shall be called wonderful, Counselor, the mighty God. The everlasting Father, the prince of peace."

My friend, there are no formulas or drugs known to mortal man that can duplicate such awesome splendor of such perfect bliss that of the *eternal God and everlasting Father.*

Why has the Lord chosen to bless me in this man- ner? God only knows. But I do know this: God says his ways are not our ways, neither are his thoughts our thoughts (Isa. 55:8).

"For as the heavens are higher than the earth, so are my ways higher than your ways, and my thoughts than your thoughts, saith the Lord," (Isa. 55:9).

To summarize these paragraphs as with the apostle Paul in Romans 11:33–34: "O the depth of the riches both of the wisdom and knowledge of God! how unsearchable are his judgments, and his ways past finding out! For who hath known the mind of the Lord? Or who hath been his counselor?"

As we continue to learn more about the wisdom and knowledge of God, I will now direct your attention to Ecclesiastes 3:10–11, 14. It reads as follows:

> I have seen the travail, which God hath given the sons of men to be exercised in it. He hath made everything beautiful in his time: also he hath set the world in their heart, so that no man can find out the work that God maketh from the beginning to the end. I know that whatsoever God doeth, it shall be forever. Nothing can be put to it, nor any thing taken from it: and God doeth it, that men should fear before him.

5

GOD WORKS IN MYSTERIOUS WAYS

As mere mortals of the human race, we have a tendency to react to persecution, criticism, and disappointments in our lives—whether it is because of sickness in our lives, the loss of a loved one, the loss of a job, failing an important test, etc.

This is a common question we often ask, *Why me?* But here, the apostle Peter is encouraging us in 1 Peter 4:12, "Beloved, think it not strange concerning the fiery trials which is to try you, as though some strange thing happened unto you."

"God works in a mysterious way, his wonders to perform" (William Cowper, 1774). Not all disappointment means the end of all good things in our lives.

As it is written in the scripture in Romans 8:28, "And we know that all things work together for good, to them that love God, to them who are called according to his purpose."

In Hebrews 12:6–7, we read: "For whom the Lord loved he chastened, and scourged every son whom he received. If ye endure chastening, God dealeth with you as with sons; for what son is he whom the father chastened not?"

"Now no chastening for the present seemed to be joyous, but grievous: nevertheless afterward it yielded the peaceable fruit of righteousness unto them which are exer- cised thereby" (Heb. 12:11).

In the midst of our trials and tribulations, things always seem to be gloom and doom. But the scripture tells us in the book of Psalms 30:5, "For his anger endured but a moment; in his favor is life: weeping may endure for a night, but joy cometh in the morning."

All these scriptures that I have quoted here to you are true and living examples of my testimony and daily walk with the Lord…and not a pontificate statement!

Let me share an experience I've had and how it cor- relates with the scripture. About a year ago, I had a dream. Whether you want to be cynical about it or not, it has spiritual and biblical implications. I will prove it to you here and now.

It's about a tremendous earthquake. I was in the house where I grew up as a child.

This earthquake was so severe! Everything was fall- ing all around me. I felt as if I was at the epicenter of this quake; yet the four walls of the house still stood without crumbling.

Despite the tremendous devastation occurring all around me, not one bone of my body was broken. Not a drop of blood was shed.

I looked outside and saw the trees swaying back and forth; the wind was boisterous. I heard the people weeping and crying. They were all discussing the earthquake. The wind and the noise continued unabated for an unusually long time.

The discussion of the people and the media pundits was about the duration and the severity of the quake and how long does an earthquake last.

During all that experience, I had not lost conscious- ness of my surroundings and was not hurt the least, even though I felt as if I was in a small boat in the middle of the ocean in the midst of a storm and tidal wave, during the aftermath of an earthquake.

While all those things were happening, I just kept praising God with these words:

"God is God. Lord, you are God! God is God." These words I kept saying repeatedly throughout the duration of the event.

All during that event, I held on firmly to my bed and would not let go, even though I looked across the other side of the room where everything seemed calm and quiet over there.

In the midst of all that rumbling and shaking, I was saying to myself, if I should let go of this security and run across to the other side of the house where everything seems to be calm and quiet, I may get hurt, or worse, get killed on my way there.

At least I felt safe right where I was despite all the dreadful things that were occurring around me.

This life experience is an example for all concerned.

Although the grass may look greener on the other side of the fence, where everything seems to be calmer, it doesn't mean that it's always better or safer over there.

We read of the example of Abram and his brother Lot. How they had to make a crucial choice as to what was best for them when they came to the crossroad of their pilgrimage out of the land of Egypt.

Lot chose the greener pastures, which lead to the green plains of Sodom and Gomorrah. Abram chose the notsogreen pasture as it may have appeared to be in the natural.

And oh, what a wise choice Abram had made, as we have seen in this example, and the end result was the marvelous act of salvation for not choosing what appears on the surface—to be green and fertile pasture, but the end result, the path to destruction.

If we really want to enjoy green pastures, let us be guided by the Word of God!

As in Psalm 23:2–3, "He maketh me to lie down in green pastures: he leadeth me beside the still waters. He restoreth my soul: he leadeth me in the paths of righteous- ness for his name's sake."

Let us choose the pasture that God chose for us, as in Ezekiel 34:14, "I will feed them in a good pasture, and upon the high mountains of Israel, shall their fold be: there shall they lie in a good fold, and in a fat pasture shall they feed upon the mountains of Israel."

"I am the door: by me if any man enter in, he shall be saved, and shall go in and out, and find pasture" (John 10:9).

There you have it!

All that our soul will ever need, the Lord has already provided for us. All we need to do is to make the right choice.

To continue this discussion on how God works in mysterious ways and how all things work together for good to them that love God, to them who are called according to his purpose, Romans 8:28 says, "We also know, through the scriptures, how some disappointment can result in unforeseen blessings in our lives."

As I described to you the earthquake experience in my life and the biblical correlation, this is what the apostle Paul has to say about his ordeal, being in a ship-wreck among prisoners, when it was determined that they should sail to Italy:

"And when it was determined that we should sail into Italy. And when the south wind blew softly, suppos- ing that they had obtained purpose, losing thence, they sailed close by Crete. But not long after there arose against it a tempestuous wind, called Euroclydon" (Acts 27:1, 13–14).

Paul's ordeal continued, as we read in verse 18, "And we being exceedingly tossed with a tempest, the next day they lightened the ship."

Verse 22: "And now I exhort you to be of good cheer: For there shall be no loss of any man's life among you, but of the ship."

Verse 30–31: "And as the shipmen were about to flee out of the ship. Paul said to the centurion and to the sol- diers, except these abide in the ship, ye cannot be saved."

Praise God! So true is this statement. Perhaps if I had ran across the house to the room on the other side, during my experience, I may not have been saved from the earthquake in my ordeal.

Being tossed in this life by disappointments, tribu- lations and distress, perplexities, earthquakes, and pesti- lence in diverse places, the only safety net we can cast our lives into and be confident in the reliance of its safety is in the hands of our Savior Jesus Christ.

Here are some other examples of testing and trials of our faith and how faith in God can calm the storms of life that tossed our souls. In Matthew 8:23–26, we read,

> And when he was entered into a ship, his disciples followed him. And, behold, there arose a great tempest in the sea, insomuch that the ship was covered with the waves: but he was asleep. And his disciples came to him, and awoke him, saying, Lord, save us: we perish. And he saith unto them, Why are ye fearful, O ye of little faith? Then he arose, and rebuked the winds and the sea; and there was a great calm.

As we continue to read in Psalm 66:10, we read, "For thou, O God, hast proved us: thou hast tried us, as silver is tried."

We read in Revelation 3:18–19, 21 as follows:

> I counsel thee to buy of me gold tried in the fire, that thou mayest be rich; and white raiment, that thou mayest be clothed, and that the shame of thy nakedness do not appear: and anoint thine eyes with eye salve, that thou mayest see. As many as I love, I rebuke and chasten: be zealous therefore, and repent. To him that overcometh will I grant to sit with me in my throne, even as I also overcame, and am set down with my Father in his throne.

Praise God! Isn't there a correlation of these scrip- tures with my testimony as I've so faithfully described it to you? I am quite sure that if you study these scriptures carefully along with my testimony, you will not have any doubts in your evaluation.

Dear friends, have you ever been in a situation where you had some strange things happened to you, and you asked yourself this question, "Lord, why me?" You have? Here is the answer to your question!

The answer is, all things work together for good to them who love God. As we read in Romans 8:28, "And we know that all things work together for good to them that love God, to them who are called according to his purpose."

Let me continue to elaborate on some of the attributes of God's mystery-working power, where the Scripture declares, "Beloved, think it not strange concern- ing the fiery trials which is to try you, as though some strange thing happened unto you" (1 Pet. 4:12).

May I refresh your memory of the Red Sea example of God's sovereign power? To the natural mind, this may seem to be a very strange way for God to deliver his people from the Egyptian army.

However, as you continue to read, I will show you why God has chosen this strange way to demonstrate his mighty power and preserve his honor.

The Word of God said, as we read in 1 Corinthians 1:27–29, "But God has chosen the foolish things of the world to confound the wise; and God hath chosen the weak things of the world to confound the things which are mighty; And base things of the world, and things which are despised, hath God chosen, yea and things which are not, to bring to nought things that are: That no flesh should glory in his presence."

Here is a perfect example of how God works in mysterious ways to demonstrate his wonderous working power through some of the strange things that happened to the people of God. We read in Exodus 14:1–4,

> And the Lord spake unto Moses, saying, Speak unto the children of Israel, that they turn and encamp before Pihahiroth, between Migdol and the sea, over against Baalzephon: before it shall ye encamp by the sea. For Pharaoh will say of the children of Israel, they are entangled in the land, the wilderness hath shut them in. And I will harden Pharaoh's heart, that he shall follow after them; and I will be honored upon Pharaoh, and upon all his host; that the Egyptians may know that I am the Lord. And they did so.

Here again we see the mysterious and strange ways through which God works and directs our lives.

To the natural mind, one would ask, why would the Lord lead his people in such a strange and difficult situation?

To the mindset of the unbelievers, they will say as Pharaoh has said, in Exodus 14:3, "For Pharaoh will say of the children of Israel, They are entangled in the land, the wilderness hath shut them in."

As you can see here, the children of Israel were fac- ing overwhelming odds against them as far as the natural mind is concerned because they had two mountains on either side of them and the Red Sea ahead of them, and the Egyptian Army pursuing after them (Exod. 14:9).

But, oh, the God of all Gods, the greatest strategist of all men of war, outflanked them. "The Lord is a man of war: the Lord is his name" (Exod. 15:3).

To continue with the discussion of the mys- tery-working power of the Lord, as concerned as we all are whenever we are faced with an extremely difficult situa- tions in our lives, when our backs are up against the wall, and there is nothing that we can do about that particular situation, let us not question God but stand still and see the salvation of the Lord.

In Ephesians 1:9, we read, "Having made known unto us the mystery of his will, according to his good plea- sure which he hath purposed in himself."

Here we read in Exodus 14:11, 13, 15–17 how God demonstrated the mystery-working power of his will to deliver the children of Israel from the Egyptian army.

> And they said unto Moses, because there were no graves in Egypt, hast thou taken us away to die in the wilderness? Wherefore hast thou dealt thus with us, to carry us forth out of Egypt? (Exod. 14:11)

> And Moses said unto the people, Fear ye not, stand still, and see the salvation of the Lord, which he will show to you today; for the Egyptians whom ye have seen today, ye shall see them no more for ever. (Exod. 14:13)

> And the Lord said unto Moses, wherefore criest thou unto me? Speak unto the children of Israel, that they go forward. But lift thou up thy rod, and stretch out thine hand over the sea, and divide it: and the children of Israel shall go on dry ground through the midst of the sea. Behold, I will harden the hearts of the Egyptians, and they shall follow them: and I will get me honor upon Pharaoh, and upon all his host, upon his chariots, and upon his horsemen. (Exod. 14:15–17)

Thank God! God is worthy to be praised with all the accolades of praise that one can utter. The Word of God said, "For them that honor me I will honor, and they that despise me shall be lightly esteemed" (1 Sam. 2:30).

We see God continues to demonstrate his mighty power to protect his holy honor, by working through his servant Moses, to fulfill his Divine will, to let Pharaoh; and all that will follow after him, know that God is God! And there is none other than the *eternal God and everlast- ing Father.*

In Exodus 14:21, we read, "And Moses stretched out his hand over the sea; and the Lord caused the sea to go back by a strong east wind all that night, and made the sea dry land, and the waters were divided."

> And the Egyptians pursued, and went in after them to the midst of the sea, even all Pharaoh's horses, his chariots, and his horsemen. (Exod. 14:23)

> And the LORD said unto Moses stretch out shine hand over the sea, that the waters may come again upon the Egyptians, upon their chariots, and upon their horsemen. (Exod. 14:26)

> And the waters returned, and cov- ered the chariots, and the horse- men, and all the host of Pharaoh that came into the sea after them; there remained not so much as

one of them. But the children of Israel walked upon dry land in the midst of the sea; and the waters were a wall unto them on their right hand, and on their left. Thus the Lord saved Israel that day out of the hand of the Egyptians. (Exod. 14:28–30)

Praise God! Here again we see the demonstration of the mighty hand of God. "The heavens declare the glory of God; and the firmament sheweth his handiwork. "Day unto day uttereth speech, and night unto night sheweth knowledge" (Ps. 19:1–2).

In Psalm 27:1–6, it reads as follows:

The Lord is my light and my salvation; whom shall I fear? The Lord is the strength of my life; of whom shall I be afraid? When the wicked, even mine enemies and even mine enemies came upon me to eat up my flesh, they stumbled and fell. Though a host should encamp against me, my heart shall not fear: though war should rise against me, in this will I be confident. One thing have I desired of the Lord, that will I seek after; that I may dwell in the house of the Lord all the days of my life, to behold the beauty of the Lord, and to inquire in his temple. For in the time of trouble he shall hide me in his pavilion: in the secret of his tabernacle shall he hide me; he shall set me up upon a rock. And now shall mine head be lifted up above mine enemies round about me; therefore will I offer in his tabernacle sacrifices of joy, I will sing, yea, I will sing praises unto the Lord.

In verse 14, the Psalmist concluded, "Wait on the Lord: be of good courage, and he shall strengthen thine heart: wait, I say, on the Lord."

To continue on with the discussion of examples of the wonder-working power of the mysteries of God, let's see what the Word of God has to say in Exodus 15:1, 9–11, 16.

> Then sang Moses and the children of Israel this song unto the Lord, and spake, saying, I will sing unto the Lord, for he hath triumphed gloriously: the horses and his rider hath he thrown into the sea. (Exod. 15:1)

> The enemy said, I will pursue, I will overtake, I will divide the spoil; my lust shall be satisfied upon them; I will draw my sword, my hand shall destroy them. (Exod. 15:9)

Isn't this the kind of threat the enemies always make against the people of God, ever since, sin entered into this world?

> Thou didst blow with thy wind, the sea covered them: they sank as lead in the mighty waters. (Exod. 15:10)

Praise God! "And the spirit of God moved upon the waters. As he did: In the beginning, when God created the heaven and the earth" (Gen. 1:2).

Exodus 15:11 continues, "Who is like unto thee, O Lord, among the gods? Who is like thee, glorious, in holi- ness, fearful in praise, doing wonders?"

> Fear and dread shall fall upon them; by the greatness of shine arm they shall be as still as a stone; till thy people pass over, O Lord, till the people pass, over, which thou hast purchased. (Exod. 15:16)

So far I have given you example after example of how far God will go to demonstrate His love for us all. The mysteries of the mercies of God are far greater than tongue or pen can ever tell. His love reaches out to the heart and soul of his people, wherever men may dwell, whether in the north, east, south, or west ends of this world. God is always near to deliver his people out of bondage.

"Greater love hath no man than this, that a man lay down his life for his friends" (John 15:13).

We have seen this example demonstrated at Calvary by Jesus Christ, the Son of the living God.

Because of this love that God has for his people, God will work in strange and mysterious ways to win the hearts and souls of those whom He loves. As the scripture has said, "Beloved, think it not strange concerning the fiery trials which is to try you, as though some strange thing happen to you" (1 Pet. 4: 12).

Some will go through the waters, some through the flood, some through earthquakes, trials, and tribulations, but all go through the blood and sovereign will of God.

We shall see as we continue to search the scripture and see what God's Word tells us concerning the testi- mony of other faithful servants of God, starting with the prophets of old and all the disciples of Christ, how faith- ful men and women throughout the ages suffered tremendously doing God's work.

We have learned of Paul and Silas's sufferings and imprisonment for no other reason but for preaching the gospel of Christ. But praise be to God for those strange, fiery trials that led to their imprisonment; nevertheless, afterward it yielded the peaceable fruits of righteousness unto salvation for the jailor and his household, as we read in Acts 16:19–31.

In dealing with the subject matter of Paul and Silas's beatings and imprisonment for the gospel's sake, a subject that is well known and preached on many times, but for the benefit of those who are not familiar with this subject, please allow me to direct you to the book of Acts 16 for details.

Here again, we witness and observe the mys- tery-working act of God by his Holy Spirit. There should be no question in our minds, however, as to how far God will go to save the hearts and souls of those whom he loved and also called.

Let's take for example when Paul desired to go to one particular place to preach the gospel but was forbid- den by the Holy Ghost to preach the Word in Asia, as we read in Acts 16:6.

In verse 9, we read, "And a vision appeared to Paul in the night:

there stood a man of Macedonia, and prayed to him, saying, Come over into Macedonia, and help us." Thank God! God's ways are not our ways, so wher-

ever the Spirit leads us, we should go without a murmur even though it may cause us imprisonment at times, as an act of obedience according to his good and perfect will, as we shall see shortly.

In Acts 16:10, we read, "And after he had seen the vision, immediately we endeavored to go into Macedonia, assuredly gathering that the Lord had called us for to preach the gospel unto them."

We see in verses 14 and 15 how a woman and her household was won by the gospel of the Kingdom of God at all costs, through Paul. This was miraculous act of sal- vation through the mystery working of the Lord. But my theme here is taken from verses 23, 26, 30, and 31.

We shall see here how a person can suffer grief and disappointment, all in the will of God, if we take it patiently. This is acceptable unto God.

Please join with me, as we read from Acts 16:23–31, and it reads as follows:

Verse 23: "And when they had laid many stripes upon them, they cast them into prison, charging the jailor to keep them safely."

Praise God! Let us examine ourselves as to how we would react if we were to find ourselves in a similar situ- ation after being sent on a mission to preach the gospel while being subjected to beating and imprisonment.

Let us learn from the heroic acts of faith as we learn from these men.

In verse 24, we read, "Who, having received such a charge, thrust them into the inner prison and made their feet in the stocks."

Let's hear of a similar situation that happened to the prophet of God, as we read in Jeremiah 20:2, and it reads, "Then Pashur smote Jeremiah the prophet, and put him in the stocks that were in the high gate of Benjamin, which was by the house of the Lord."

Again, we are reminded of the admonitions given to us as concerning the fiery trial, which is to try us as though some strange thing happened to us.

We shall see as we read from Acts 16:25, "And at midnight, Paul and Silas prayed, and sang praises unto God: and the prisoners heard them.

And suddenly there was a great earthquake, so that the foundations of the prison were shaken: and immediately all the doors were opened, and every one's bands were loosed."

Thank God for the power of prayer that breaks the bands of prison yoke. Remember what I've told you about my earthquake experience, where not a bone of my body was broken and not a drop of my blood was shed. The God who protected Paul and Silas during their earthquake experience is the same God who protected me.

Great is our God! How great the things he has done for me. Let's continue on to Acts 16:27–30, and it reads as follows:

And the keeper of the prison awaking out of his sleep, and seeing the prison doors open, he drew out his sword, and would have killed himself, supposing that the prisoners had fled. But Paul cried with a loud voice, say- ing, do thyself no harm: for we are all here. Thank the Lord, for his Divine plan of salvation, to whosoever will accept it freely! Then he called for a light, and sprang in and came trembling, and fell down before Paul and Silas. And brought them out, and said, Sirs, what must I do to be saved?

Again we see God's plan of salvation at work! As we read in Matthew 7:7–8, "Ask, and it shall be given you; seek, and ye shall find; knock, and it shall be opened unto you. For every one that asked received; and he that seeketh findeth; and to him that knocked it shall be opened."

As we continue from Acts 16:30–31, we read: "Sirs, what must I do to be saved? And they said, Believe on the Lord Jesus Christ, and thou shalt be saved, and thy house."

Praise God for the peaceable fruits of righteousness that has been yielded here after those chastening experi- ence by Paul and Silas, beating and imprisonment.

The foregoing examples have confirmed the cor- relation with the word of God that said: "All things work together for good to them that love God, to them who are the called according to his purpose" (Rom. 8:28).

Also in 1 Peter 4:12, "We have the conformation of the word, that reads thus: Beloved, think it not strange concerning the fiery trial which is to try you, as though some strange thing happened unto you."

6

WHAT IS A TESTIMONY?

Now concerning testimony, what is a *testimony*?

1. A declaration of affirmation of fact or truth, as that given before a court
2. Evidence in support of a fact or assertion; proof
3. The collective written and spoken testimony offered in a legal case
4. A public declaration regarding a religious experience

Others define it as something that serves as tangible verification.

In John 3:26, 32–33, we read likewise, "And they came unto John, and said unto him, Rabbi, he that was with thee beyond Jordan, to whom thou barest witness, behold, the same baptizeth, and all men come to him.... And what he hath seen and heard, that he testified; and no man received his testimony. He that hath received his testimony hath set to his seal that God is true."

From the blood of righteous Abel (Hebrews 11:4) all the way down to John the Baptist and all others that follow, many have sealed their testimony with their lives for what they believe and know to be true.

This testimony is real. I do not only believe that it is real; I know that it is real by the evidence, which I have given you. I aver it with absolute certainty!

Oh, but do not conclude that my entire Christian walk with the Lord has always been just glorious dreams and visions from the Lord.

The Bible said, "To whom much is given, much is required" (Luke 12:48).

Don't you realize that the devil has not just stood by in awe with his hand over his mouth, wondering what to do about me?

The devil's desire is to sift me as wheat is sifted. So desired he of Peter! As we read in Luke 22:31, "And the Lord said, Simon, Simon, behold, Satan hath desired to have you, that he may sift you as wheat."

Throughout my life and my daily walk with the Lord, I have suffered many trials, tribulations, and disap- pointments too numerous to mention.

But through it all, I have learned to trust in Jesus.

I've learned to depend upon his word.

The Bible said, "Beloved, think it not strange con- cerning the fiery trial which is to try you, as though some strange thing happened unto you" (1 Pet. 4:12).

As of June 1995: My Sunday school teacher, casti- gated me, a brother whom we have mutual respect regard- ing a statement made by him: I didn't acquiesce and asked for scripture clarification from him.

His trenchant retort was humiliating and insulting to me in the presence of all. I had to leave the church because he refused to reconcile with me even though I sincerely made an effort to reconcile with him. However, like the apostle Paul, I counted it all but loss, for Christ.

Jesus and his disciples were publicly humiliated; his disciples were persecuted, and so were the prophets of old. My minor persecution is pale in comparison.

In spite of all those things, I am blessed. I am blessed!

Thank God I am blessed.

When I am troubled by trials and tribulations in this world, I take solace with the words of the apostle Paul in Romans 8:18, "For I reckon that the sufferings of this present time are not worthy to be compared with the glory which shall be revealed in us."

> Who shall separate us from the love of Christ? Shall tribulation, or distress, persecution, or famine, or nakedness, or peril, or sword? As it is written, for thy sake we are killed all the day long; we are accounted as sheep for the slaughter. Nay, in all these things we are more than conquerors through him that loved us. For I am persuaded, that neither death, nor life, nor angels, nor principalities, nor powers, nor things present, nor things to come, Nor height, nor depth, nor any other creature, shall be able to separate us from the love of God, which is in Christ Jesus our Lord. (Rom. 8:35–39)

Praise God! All these verses I've committed to memory, written indelibly upon the tablets of my heart.

When I think of Calvary, the cross of which Jesus bore for my sins, the agony and suffering of which he bled and died, I draw from the wealth of the Word of God, which says, "Wherefore seeing we also are compassed about with so great a cloud of witnesses, let us lay aside every weight, and the sins which cloth so easily beset us, and let us run with patience the race that is set before us. Looking unto Jesus the author and finisher of our faith" (Heb. 12:1–2).

When conflict and strife seem to be the order of the day, again I draw from the wealth of the word of God that says, "Follow peace with all men, and holiness, without which no man shall see the Lord; Looking diligently lest any man fail of the grace of God; lest any root of bit- terness springing up troubled you, and thereby many be defiled" (Heb. 12:14–15).

All twenty-nine verses I've committed to memory from my youth, written indelibly upon the tablets of my heart.

As I grew and learned to lean on Jesus, I studied the Holy Scripture fervently like David the Psalmist! In Psalm 42:1, "As the hart panteth after the water brooks, so pan- teth my soul after thee, O God."

As I developed this hunger and thirst after righ- teousness, I studied the Word of God diligently to let God's word be my guide as a lamp to my feet and a light unto my pathway so that I can share with any man who will ask of my faith and what it means to be born again.

Like what Jesus answered to Nicodemus, "Except a man be born again, he cannot see the kingdom of God. That which is born of the flesh is flesh, and that which is born of the Spirit is Spirit. The wind bloweth where it listeth, and thou hearest the sound thereof, but canst not tell whence it cometh, and whither it goeth: so is every one that is born of the Spirit" (John 3:3, 6, 8). All thir- ty-six verses I've committed to memory from my youth, written indelibly upon the tablets of my heart.

In reference to sin and grace, when temptation comes my way, I asked myself this question, "How can I do this great wickedness and sin against my God?" Again I draw from the wealth of the Word of God, which says, "What shall we say then? Shall we continue in sin, that grace may abound? God forbid. How shall we that are dead to sin, live any longer therein?" (Rom. 6:1–2).

The Word of God said, "What fruit had ye then in those things whereof ye are now ashamed? For the end of those things is death" (Rom. 6:21). All twenty-three verses I've committed to memory from my youth to this day. Praise God.

For we all have sinned and come short of the glory of God. We have sinned in words, deeds, thoughts, and actions. That's why we need to confess our sins daily before the Lord.

When I need to renew my vows unto the Lord and to be free from the burdens of temptations, I take solace in the Word of God, as in Psalm 139, "O Lord, thou hast searched me, and know me. Thou knowest my downsitting and mine uprising; thou understandest my thought afar off. Thou compassest my path and my lying down, and art acquainted with all my ways. For there is not word in my tongue, but, lo, O Lord, thou knowest it altogether" (Ps. 139:1–4). All twentyfour verses I've com- mitted to memory from my youth.

I take great pleasure in delighting myself in the Lord. I let the Word of God be my guide as a lamp to my feet and a light to my pathway in my daily walk with the Lord.

My life is a living testimony to everyone who knows me.

The Bible says, "How beautiful upon the mountains are the feet of him that bringeth good tidings, that publish peace; that bringeth good tidings of good, that published salvation; that saith unto Zion, Thy God reigneth" (Isa. 52:7). All fifteen verses I've committed to memory from my youth. Praise God.

Jesus said, "Seek ye first the kingdom of God, and his righteousness; and all these things shall be added unto you" (Matt. 6:33).

My testimony, which I have given you here, bears record of that fact. From the very early age of seventeen, I have devoted my life to Jesus. It was during that period of my young adolescent years that I studied these scriptures and many other chapters and verses of the Bible I have committed to memory, even to this very day and always will.

While there are others of my peers who may have gone on to pursue higher education, I used what was available to me at that time. And that was the freedom to study the Word of God, of which I have no regrets!

Perhaps if I had the privilege and the opportunity to pursue a college education at that time, my circumstances would have been much different in my life, and the Lord would not have blessed me in the spiritual manner in which I have been blessed.

7

Short Biography

As I recall, I've made a promise early on in the intro- duction of my testimony and brief chronology of my family history and my childhood experience that I would explain a little about my later years and life accomplishments.

But first, after all those events took place in my ado- lescent years, I went to work in Kingston, the capital city of Jamaica, West Indies. There, a dear Christian cousin of mine helped me to get situated in the city and also got me living accommodations.

Another Christian brother loaned me some fur- nished arrangements.

My cousin was very instrumental in helping me to find a job. He and his wife also provided me with some homecooked meals. Another Christian brother allowed me to use his furniture temporarily.

Through many trials and tribulations, I was still able to live a godly life there in the city. One experience is worth mentioning here.

I got a job in a very prestigious hotel in the city, working for pittance wages, midnight to 8:00 a.m., along with another Christian brother from the country, who was staying there with me even though I had told him that jobs were very hard to get in the city at that time. However, one day, he came to stay with me unannounced. One night while we were working together in the kitchen of the hotel (there was always plenty of food there in the kitchen), the vice president of the hotel came and invited me up to his hotel suite to do some work for him. After, I went up to his suite! While I was there working, he introduced me to his private suite men's room. It was there that he made sexual advances toward me.

Like Joseph in Potiphar's house in Egypt, I got out of that hotel as fast as I could and have not returned to that job.

My Christian brother did remain on the job. He stayed on the job and worked, ate, and got fat.

Occasionally he would bring me home some food, but after a while, he would brag about it even to the point of putting his feet on me as his footstool and told me that if only I had stayed on the job, I would get as healthy and fat as he. However, I counted all those things but loss, for Christ.

I finally immigrated to Toronto, Canada. I spent a year in Toronto and then decided to come to the USA.

But before I immigrated to the USA, one day while I was out job hunting way out in the outskirts of Toronto, while I was being interviewed for the job, the interviewer told me that the position was already filled.

On my way out from the interview, I met this young Caucasian man who was waiting to be interviewed for the same job. I waited in the waiting room until he was fin- ished. I then asked him if he had got the job. He told me the only reason why he did not get the job was because he spoke very little English.

I realized it was because of the color of my skin why I did not get the job.

I left feeling very disappointed. I walked to the bus stop and waited there a long time for the bus to come. It was very cold and snowy that day. So cold, after waiting for the bus a very long time, I started to get very panicky and almost to the point of being frostbitten.

I was saying in my mind, Lord, if I should freeze here to death, it would be seen as being rejected because of my race. Soon thereafter, along came a pickup truck, which stopped by the bus stop; the driver was a white man! God bless his soul. He gave me a ride all the way into the city, took me into a restaurant and bought me coffee and doughnuts.

Again I say, "May God richly bless his soul."

"God is our refuge and strength, a very present help in trouble" (Ps. 46:1).

Good people come in all colors and in all races.

Incidentally, not too long ago, I was able to return a similar charitable deed to a young Caucasian man when my wife and I were returning from Toronto, Canada, on an Amtrak train.

There we met this young Caucasian man who was returning home from a tennis tournament.

As we sat together at the dining room table after we had finished eating, there was some leftover food that we did not want. The young man asked us if he could have it. We told him it was okay for him to have it.

At another sitting while my wife and I sat and ate, I suggested to my wife that it would be nice for us to buy some food to take back to this young man, which we did. The young man was very appreciative for the food.

In closing this saga of my testimony, I said all that to say this: When someone helps you in a lifesaving situ- ation, you have a tendency never to forget it. And there- fore, you will always render kindness to someone in need. After living in Toronto, Canada, for about one year,

I came to New York City in 1967.

I went to vocational trade school and graduated with a diploma in gas and electric welding. I also learned other phases of welding, including MIG welding.

During the succeeding years, I fell in love with a very lovely Christian young lady. We got engaged, got married soon thereafter, and had two lovely daughters.

I studied and acquired a high school education from American School High School, Chicago. I graduated with an academic diploma.

In pursuit of continuing education, I continued to broaden my horizon and increase my overall knowledge by taking a correspondence course with National Technical School of Los Angeles. I graduated with a master course in color television electronics.

I continued on in a correspondence course with Cleveland Institute of Electronics as an electronics technician.

Through further studies, I was able to acquire my FCC General Radiotelephone First Class Operator License with Radar Endorsement. I also completed a broadcast and data communication correspondence course and a lab experiment and design correspondence course from Heathkit Zenith Educational Systems.

In spite of all my works and labor of love and a desire to broaden my horizon and increase my overall knowledge, my present job status is not exactly what I wanted it to be. I do know however that in order to achieve ones goal in life, he or she has to brake from their creative chrysalis to achieve the recognition they deserve. Similar to the Apostle Paul, however, "Not that I speak in respect of want: for I have learned, in whatsoever state I am, therewith to be content" (Phil. 4:11).

Even though I have not reached the acme of my career, I have learned from Paul's example to be content in whatsoever state or situation I am in, whether in the state of satisfaction of accomplishment in my career goals, or job dissatisfaction, etc. I have learned to be in the state of contentment! Thank God.

8

Faith in Action

In Matthew 14:25–31, we read,

> And in the fourth watch of the night Jesus went unto them, walking on the sea. And when the disciples saw him walking on the sea, they were troubled, saying, it is a spirit; and they cried out for fear. But strait way Jesus spake unto them, saying, be of good cheer, it is I; be not afraid. And Peter answered him and said, Lord, if it be thou bid me come unto thee on the water. And he said, come. And when Peter was come down out of the ship, he walked on the water, to go to Jesus. But when he saw the wind boister- ous, he was afraid; and beginning to sink, he cried, saying, Lord, save me. And immediately Jesus stretched forth his hand, and caught him, and said unto him, O thou of little faith, wherefore didst thou doubt?

All thirtysix verses I've studied and committed to memory from my youth.

If Peter had kept his eyes on Jesus and not on the boisterous conditions around him, he would not have started to sink. This is a clear example for us Christians today! If we want to walk with Jesus, we must keep our eyes on him and not on the circumstances around us.

Yes, dark clouds may rise and strong winds may blow, but if we put our trust in God and keep our eyes on Jesus, he will calm the troubled waters and we will never sink hopelessly because "on Christ, the solid rock, I stand; All other ground is sinking sand" (Edward Mote, 1834).

Habakkuk 2:4 admonishes us, "The just shall live by faith." We also read in Matthew 8:8–10 how Jesus marveled at the centurion's faith. In verse 10, we read, "When Jesus heard it, he marveled, and said to them that followed, Verily I say unto you, I have not found so great faith, no, not in Israel."

As God has given to every man a measure of faith, however, my measure of faith may not measure up to this centurion's faith, as described here. Each individual situ- ation is unique.

For example, I may choose to resolve certain conflicts in my own life, for example, such as applying the principle of turning the other cheek, whereas another person may choose to use the sword as Peter has demonstrated when they arrested Christ in the garden of Gethsemane.

Although, not attributing the turning of one's cheek as a sign of weakness, but as an act of faith by letting Christ fight my battle, who do you think will be the ulti- mate victor? The peacemaker through Christ, of course!

A perfect example can be pointed out here. No one can ever accuse Jesus Christ as being a weakling even though the scripture said, "He was oppressed, and he was afflicted, yet he opened not his mouth: he is brought as a lamb to the slaughter, and as a sheep before her shearers is dumb, so he opened not his mouth" (Isa. 53:7).

In other instances of scourging and cruel mocking, he did not fight back, yet he was all God and man, perfect in all his ways and perfect in the will of the Father.

Moses of the Old Testament, we are told, was the meekest man on earth yet so strong in leadership that the world will never forget.

On numerous occasions in my own life, I applied the principle of faith in action.

Even though I might not have gotten the victory right away each and every time, however, the end result has always been victorious. You too can apply the same principle and become a daily winner through faith in action.

My faith, as small as a mustard seed as it may be, in my obedience to his calling and his answer to my prayer, when I asked the Lord to have mercy on my soul—and his smiling face I have seen—leads me to believe there is no distance in prayer; the prayer of faith can also save you too. I cannot promise you that your salvation experience will be the same as mine. God is the only one who can determine an individual's salvation process.

In Matthew 9:28–29, Jesus asked the blind men who came to him, "Believe ye that I am able to do this? They said unto him, yea, Lord. Then touched he their eyes, saying, According to your faith be it unto you."

Thank you, God, for the blessings in Jesus I find when by faith I accepted the Lord Jesus as my personal savior.

When I was a sinner, wretched, naked, and spir- itually blind (myopic), this same Jesus, eternally in the Heavens, spiritually asked of me a similar question while I was on my knees praying and asking the Lord to have mercy upon my soul. When he heard me from his holy heaven, a miraculous act of salvation took place in my life; I have never been the same since. How marvelous a salvation Christ has for everyone who believes and asks his forgiveness?

In Romans 6:17–18, we read in this wise, "But God be thanked, that ye were the servants of sin, but ye have obeyed from the heart that form of doctrine which was delivered you. Being then made free from sin, ye became the servants of righteousness."

Have I heeded to the Word of God and obeyed his call? I thanked God, I have! Ever since I was a child, I always had a burning desire to serve the Lord since that Tuesday afternoon of 1964, when my faith reached out to the Lord, in my moments of despair, and he heard me from his throne of mercy and saved me and smiled to me with love, mercy, compassion, and forgiveness of sins. He can do the same for you! God is no respecter of persons. His love transcends all races, all colors, and all boundaries. In Romans 6:18, we read in this wise, "Being then made free from sin, ye became servants of righteousness." I thank the Lord for his grace and the faith I find through Jesus, who has cleansed me and made me whole by his blood and righteousness.

I was a sinner, deep in the mire of sin, until I called on the name of the Lord in my despair. The good Lord heard me when I called on his name, to have mercy on my soul, then he heard me and saved me from the brink of suicide into his holy presence.

James, in his epistles, writes, "My brethren, count it all joy when ye fall into divers temptations; Knowing this, that the trying of your faith worketh patience."

I am a living witness to this truth that on many occasions in my own life, my faith has been tried in such a way only the good Lord can explain.

Case in point, even during the time of my writing this book, the opposition from the enemy to it being pub- lished has been relentless.

Not too long ago, I was speaking to a Christian brother in the ministry. During our conversation, the subject of my book came up. While we were encouraging each other on the work we are doing in the service of the Lord, prior to our conversation, there was no interruption on the communication links between our phone lines. No sooner than when we began discussing ways of combating the enemy, immediately our conversation was interrupted by a considerable amount of static. As we suggested using the medium of prayer to break the stronghold of the enemy, the phone lines went completely dead, confirming my testimony.

Within seconds of the telephone interruptions, the brother called me back to continue the conversation. This time, there was no static. We laughed respectfully at the irony of the situation, after which we continued with our conversation and then concluded with prayer.

The incident I had just described to you concerning the trying of my faith is just one of many obstacles the devil has amassed against me, trying to prevent me from writing this book.

Temptations, discouragement, and disappointments presented themselves in many ways, as seen on TV every day, which seems to be the norm of society today. But "who shall separate us from the love of Christ? Shall tribu- lation, or distress, or persecution, or famine, or nakedness, or peril, or sword?" (Rom. 8:35).

There is the public perception that today's main- stream society is more interested in sex, violence, fiction, new age religion, and the occult and want very little to do with anything of religious matters. "But as for me and my house, we will serve the Lord!" (Josh. 24:15).

It is declared in 1 Peter 2:20, "For what glory is it, if when ye be buffeted for your faults, ye shall take it patiently? But if, when ye do well, and suffer for it, ye take it patiently, this is acceptable with God."

There have been many occasions in my own life in which I have performed good deeds and have suffered for doing so, confirming Peter's declaration as stated above.

For example, many years ago, after I graduated from Radio Television Electronics School, I was young, very eager to learn, and acquired some muchneeded handson electronics experience. A former coworker, a friend of mine, introduced me to an electronics friend of his who, at that time, owned a radio and TV service shop.

After personally building several pieces of electron- ics test equipment of my own, I would occasionally stop by this young man's electronics service shop, hoping that I could learn something from a pro in the business.

I offered to lend him one or two pieces of my test equipment to perform some electronics test on a piece of equipment he was working on. In exchange he allowed me to watch him perform some of those tests.

Unfortunately, he performed all of those tests with- out allowing me to observe his performance to learn some of the techniques of the trade from him while using my test equipment. How is that for doing good deeds and suffering disappointment for doing so? However, I took it patiently and counted it all but loss, for Christ. This, I believe, is acceptable unto the Lord, with regard to my suffering!

I honestly believe that if I was one of his drink- ing buddies, he would not have any problem having me around him, but because I was not, ostracism from friends and wouldbe friends is a price we as

Christians have to pay for being in this world but not of this world, as Christ has warned us in John 15:17–19.

In other occurrences, I found myself in a job situa- tion where I was literally harassed and my faith tested so severely to the point that I had to resign from that job. Quite naturally, I could stay there and legally fight the battle for my job. But the battle was not mine to fight but Christ alone.

We are reminded of the Word of God that said, "If when you do well, and you suffer for it, you take it patiently, this is acceptable with God" (1 Pet. 2:20).

This is what happened to me during my six-month's stay on that job. I was harassed, ridiculed, and ostracized by my former coworkers. Ironically, the most severe test of my faith including these and other trying experiences came from apostate Christian brothers, who had lost their first love.

The experience I had on that job is the antithesis of peaceful coexistence among fellow employees. The work environment became so deplorable, I finally decided to leave the job by writing a formal letter of resignation to the department of personnel through my then immediate supervisor and superintendent without naming any of my persecutors.

Would you believe that nothing was ever done about my complaints even long after I resigned from that job? It wasn't until after a few weeks had passed when the depart- ment of personnel kept writing to me, wanting to know the reasons for my not returning to work and to state my reasons through formal resignation.

I finally did my own investigation and found out that my letter of resignation never got past the superinten- dent's file even though my letter wasn't cavil by any stretch of the imagination.

It is not my purpose or intention then or now to spill my guts of all the trials and tribulations that occurred in my life. However, based on adverse situation, in terms of disappointments and the many obstacles that I have encountered during the process of writing this book and by editorial critiques, I have been told by some editors that these and other heartrending stories are what most readers want to hear. However, for the greater good of my testimony and to all concerned, knowing that the good far outweighs the bad, it is my earnest desire that truth and goodness will prevail, and my testimony will go forward and touch the hearts and lives of all who read it. Continuing with the examples of faith in action, in the Bible we read, "So then faith cometh by hearing, and hearing by the word of God" (Rom. 10:17).

I was a sinner, raised in a home where my father, being a deacon of his church, taught me the fear of the Lord, not really being born again; however, it was through hearing and hearing of the Word of God, I believe, that led to my salvation during my young adolescence years, of which I am so grateful. Like Simeon, the man of God, and all the believers of his day including all the believers of our time and as many as the Lord our God shall call.

As we have seen the prophetic prophecies of the Word of God come to pass concerning the birth of our Lord and Savior Jesus Christ found in Luke 2:11, 18–20, 27–30, which reads as follows: "For unto you is born this day in the city of David a Savior, which is Christ the Lord."

Verse 18–20: "And all they that heard it wondered at those things which were told them by the shepherds. But Mary kept all these things, and pondered them in her heart. And the shepherds returned, glorifying and prais- ing God for all the things that they heard and seen, as it was told them" Here we have these shepherds praising and glorifying God for what they have seen and heard! Why should I be lethargic in my response in sharing with you what God has blessed me with?

"So then, as you have seen the evidence of the Scripture, as it is written. Faith cometh by hearing, and hearing of the word of God" (Rom. 10:17). It was through the hearing of the Word of God, through prophecies and faith in the written Word of God, why they were able to believe the evidence when they saw the scripture fulfilled right before their eyes. It is imperative that we believe God for what he says and for who he is! He is Lord *eternal*!

We are reminded through scriptures in Ephesians 2:8–9, "For by grace are ye saved through faith; and that not of yourselves: it is the gift of God. Not of works, lest any man should boast."

I am a living witness to this stated fact, as I have stated earlier in my writing. This is not hyperbole by any stretch of the imagination. I am merely emphasizing the truth!

In Romans 6:18, we read in this wise, "Being then made free from sin, ye became servants of righteousness."

I am personally grateful to the Lord for his grace and mercy, who has forgiven me of my sins, cleansed me, and made me whole by his blood and righteousness, through faith in Christ our Lord.

God is no respecter of persons. What he has done for me, he will do for you—with open arms, and he will pardon you, cleanse you, and make you whole!

My fellow readers, including myself and those of the household of faith, no matter what the situation or cir- cumstances that we may face in this life, it behooves us as soldiers in the army of the Lord to put on the whole armor of God—having the shield of faith, the helmet of salvation, the breastplate of righteousness, and the sword of the spirit—and fight the good fight of faith and lay hold on eternal life.

So that when we come to the end of our Christian sojourn here on this earth, we may say with the Apostle Paul, "I have fought a good fight. I have finished my course. I have kept the faith."

"Henceforth there is laid up for me a crown of righ- teousness, which the Lord, the righteous judge, shall give me at that day: and not to me only, but unto all them also that love his appearing" (2 Tim. 4:7–8).

Since Jesus saved me, in my daily walk with him, the enemy of my soul is always accusing me before the Lord; therefore, I am fighting the good fight of faith—not a physical fight, however, but a spiritual warfare against the common enemy, the devil.

Sometimes we may feel discouraged and think that our work is in vain, but the psalmist David tells us to wait on the Lord. "Be of good courage, and he shall strengthen shine heart: wait I say on the Lord" (Ps. 27:14).

I am living by this principle every day, ever since I met the Savior of my soul! You, too, by faith can live a life of victory by faith in Jesus Christ.

In (Isa. 41:10), we read, "Fear thou not; for I am with thee: be not dismayed; for I am thy God: I will strengthen thee; yea I will help thee;

yea I will uphold thee with the right hand of my righteousness." God said it, and I believe it with all my heart.

With the thoughts of these promises in mind and our strength renewed, let us keep our hopes alive with these encouraging words from the scripture that reads as follows: "But as it is written, Eye hath not seen, nor ear heard, neither have entered into the heart of man, the things which God hath prepared for them that love him" (1 Cor. 2:9).

Praise God! Doesn't this make you want to be absent from this body and to be present with the Lord? Here is what the apostle Paul has to say about this, "For I am in a strait betwixt two, having a desire to depart, and to be with Christ, which is far better: Nevertheless to abide in the flesh is more needful for you" (Phil. 1:23, 24).

In 2 Corinthians 5:2–4, 8–10, Paul continued to say, "For in this we groan, earnestly desiring to be clothed upon with our house which is from heaven: If so be that being clothed we shall not be found naked. For we that are in this tabernacle do groan, being burdened: not for that we would be unclothed, but clothed upon, that mor- tality might be swallowed up of life.

"We are confident I say and willing rather to be absent from the body, and to be present with the Lord. Wherefore we labor, that, whether present or absent, we may be accepted of him. For we must all appear before the judgment seat of Christ; that everyone may receive the things done in his body, according to that he hath done, whether it be good or bad."

As for my desire and me after this written testimony of mine is made known to the world and Jesus is lifted up, God is glorified and some soul is won for the kingdom of God through my testimony.

I pray that I take heed to myself lest I win others for the kingdom, and I myself be a castaway (1 Cor. 9:27).

Therefore I can say like Simeon, the man of God, in Luke 2:29–30, "Lord, now lettest thou thy servant depart in peace, according to thy word: For mine eyes have seen thy salvation."

9

FINAL APPEAL

In my final thoughts, please hear these words, "Jesus is coming soon!" How soon, you may ask?

Jesus tells us in Matthew 24:36, "But of that day and hour knoweth no man, no, not the angels of heaven, but my Father only."

However, the scripture clearly gives us enough knowledge and information to know the time and season of his coming.

Let's hear some of the signs Jesus said will take place prior to his Second Coming. Jesus said in Matthew 24:32, "Now learn a parable of the fig tree; when his branches is yet tender, and putted forth leaves, ye know that summer is nigh."

Let's turn our attention again, back to verses 7 and 8, and it reads as follows: "For nation shall rise against nation, and kingdom against kingdom: and there shall be famines, and pestilences, and earthquakes, in divers places. All these are the beginning of sorrows."

Is there anyone reading this book today who has not seen any of these signs?

You may shrug your shoulders in disbelief and say, "Have I not heard these things before? And yet, I've not seen his return." You may continue to say, "From when I was a child, I've been hearing about Christ coming, and he has not returned yet."

Well, my friend! Perhaps so said the people of Lot's day. They thought that they could indulge in their sinful lifestyles as long as their idea of time was concerned, not expecting God's visitation of wrath upon them suddenly. Until God rained down fire and brimstone upon them, as we read in Genesis 19:24–30.

In verse 24, we read, "Then the Lord rained upon Sodom and upon Gomorrah brimstone and fire from the Lord out of heaven." For those who are not familiar with this event in history, the Bible said of Lot, "His wife and two daughters, escaped." However, in verse 26, "We have seen that Lot's wife looked back from behind him, and she became a pillar of salt."

Likewise, the people of Noah's day, when Noah warned the people of the coming flood, they mocked him and laughed at him and his family until the flood came and destroyed them all, saving Noah and his family only.

My friend! The people of Sodom and Gomorrah had their day. The people of Noah's time had their day. Our day is coming.

For the righteous, it will be a day of redemption.

Oh, what a day of rejoicing that will be for the saints of God. When we all see Jesus, we will sing and shout for victory!

For the sinners and the ungodly, it will be weep- ing and wailing and gnashing of teeth and an eternal separation from the living God. But there is hope while Jesus is still pleading mercy! Don't wait until tomorrow.

Tomorrow may be too late. Come to Jesus now is my plea to you!

Dear readers, you may say that you are not ready. "Jesus is not here yet, and I have plenty of time." I would not bet on that if I were you. Please do not be deceived. Jesus said, "Heaven and earth shall pass away, but my words shall not pass away" (Matt. 24:35).

If in doubt, read Ezekiel 12:21–22, 25, 27–28. Verse 21–22 says, "And the word of the Lord came unto me, saying, Son of man, what is that proverb that ye have in the land of Israel, saying, The days are prolonged, and every vision failed?"

> For I am the Lord: I will speak, and the word that I shall speak shall come to pass; it shall be no more prolonged: for in your days, O rebellious house, will I say the word, and will perform it, saith the Lord God. (Ezek. 12:25)

> Son of man, behold, they of the house of Israel say, The vision that he seethe is far many days to come, and he prophesied of the times that are far off. Therefore say unto them, thus saith the Lord God; There shall none of my words be prolonged any more, but the word which I have spoken shall be done, saith the Lord God. (Ezek. 12:27–28)

The prophet Ezekiel wrote the words I have just quoted above, taken from Ezekiel 12:21–22, 25, 27–28, as a declaration from God. Whether you believe it or not is your affair. God said it, and I believe it! The rest is up to you to believe it. But believe it or not, the day of reckon- ing is closer than you think!

The coming of the Lord is not too far away, and the only thing that can save mankind is to be washed in the blood of Jesus and be cleansed from all our sins!

But we must first repent of our sins and confess Jesus as Lord of all!

Allow me to share this experience with you. It was on a Monday afternoon of December 30, 1996, while I was asleep, before preparing to go to work.

In my sleep, I dreamt that I was on a large boat on the waters around Manhattan, New York City, when sud- denly I heard a mysterious noise like a whirlwind coming from the sky above.

While being terrified by such strange sound, I looked up toward the sky, and there I saw this giant mete- orite falling toward the earth with accelerating speed. As it entered the earth's atmosphere with great speed and thundering noise, it was like another planet was about to collide with planet Earth.

Everyone was crying out in fear and panic, saying, "A meteorite is going to hit the earth." As it got closer and closer toward the earth, it fell horrifically in the river along Battery Park, New York City.

The impact of the meteorite hitting the water was awesome. It resulted in huge tidal waves that caused the boat to lose control erratically, and it began to sink.

As the waves swept across the deck of the boat, strong gushes of water rushed over the piers, onto the land.

Everyone around me was crying out in fear. I thanked the Lord despite the awareness of myself not knowing how to swim, and death appeared imminent.

I remained steadfast in my seat. I held on to my wife's hand real tight, having the "peace of God, which passeth all understanding, shall keep our hearts and minds through Christ Jesus" (Phil. 4:7). I was praying to the Lord, with these words, "Lord, into thy hand I commit my spirit. Have mercy on my soul."

Having the assurance, it is well with my soul— despite the people all around us being filled with fear and panic and running to and fro for their lives. As for my concern, I was overwhelmed with peace and assurance of the inner peace in my heart as if I was on the sea of tran- quility, knowing that to be absent from the body is to be present with the Lord. As stated in 2 Corinthians 5:8, "We are confident, I say, and willing rather to be absent from the body, and to be present with the Lord."

While the siege continued, it was as if massive pieces of concrete slabs were also falling from the sky.

Some of the huge slabs of concrete had strange inscriptions written on them—as if written in the lan- guage of ancient times.

Immediately, after the meteorite hit the water and debris continued to fall, appeared in the sky some kind of strange military gun ship spraying the shorelines and piers with rapid machinegun fire, which had everyone in a state of panic while they cried out for fear.

Soon afterward, when the tidal wave was quies- cent and the gun ship bombardments ceased for a brief moment, the boat docked safely along the pier.

But when the enemy saw us getting off the boat to safety into a narrow passageway, another strange militarytype gun ship suddenly appeared in the sky with deadly assault on us, as if to say, "Okay, you think you are going to get away freely—we do have the capability to smoke you out."

The bombardment continued unabated, this time with billows of smoke as if coming from the mouth of a dragon, shooting at us, trying to prevent us from escaping. We ran into this narrow passageway to escape the onslaught of the attackers, but the enemy kept shooting at us.

As this relentless siege continued, we entered safely into another small passageway only to be hindered by a strange dragon-like creature— killing and committing acts of mayhem to everyone who tried to escape his vicious attack.

As I saw the viciousness of that strange monster-look- ing beast, I hid myself in a cleft of that passageway, not wanting to draw his attention to where I was hiding.

Soon afterward, I saw one of my brothers approach- ing that same passageway. I tried, however, to draw his attention away from the danger ahead, which would only lead to his destruction.

I finally escaped that heinous carnage by exiting carefully through a safe egress.

I thank God for the victory! In Revelation 12:1–6, 13–17, the Bible tells us how the dragon tried to destroy the woman and her child—but did not prevail.

God provided a way of escape for the woman and her child. The Bible said, "And she brought forth a man child, who was to rule all nations with a rod of iron; and her child was caught up unto God, and to his throne" (Rev. 12:5).

"God is our refuge and strength, a very present help in trouble" (Ps. 46:1).

Throughout the beginning of time, the devil has always tried to subvert God's plan of salvation by any means he can but to no avail.

In Revelation 12:4–6, we read of the woman and her child escaping the fury of the dragon by the provi- dence of the Lord preparing a place of God in the wilder- ness for her, where she hath a place prepared of

God, that they should feed her there a thousand and two hundred and three score days.

We do know, however, the outcome of the miraculous event in history, how Christ won the victory at Calvary over Satan. That wicked serpent called the devil. "He shall bruise our head. But we through Christ shall bruise his heel" (Gen. 3:15; Rom. 16:20).

Although I do not have a biblical correlation for this particular experience, I do know this, however, the Bible said, "But if the watchman see the sword come, and blow not the trumpet, and the people be not warned; if the sword come, and take any person from among them, he is taken away in his iniquity; but his blood will I require at the watchman's hand" (Ezek. 33:6).

As strange and paradoxical as this experience may seem, the morals of this paradox is this: I thank my God that no matter what kind of situation I may find myself in—whither in my walking, in my talking, in my sleeping, or in my waking—I thank my Lord for the praise of God in my heart and on my lips.

I am by no means claiming to be anyone but a humble child of God. I am not making any predictions or prophesying anything or pontificating.

But to the people of New York City, ask yourselves this question: Are we better than those people in other cities and states who are experiencing natural disasters all around this great country of ours, and the rest of the world, for that matter? Think about it carefully before you dismiss this information as mere folly.

The only biblical explanation that I can give for this allegorical statement at this time is found in one of Paul's letters to the Corinthians that reads likewise. But I speak this by permission, and not of commandment" (1 Cor. 7:6). However, let every man discern the times in which we are now living in; these are evil times. To the people of the world, however, they may see it as fun times, not discerning, as Christ has warned in Luke 12:56.

As I have stated to you before, my experiences with the Lord cannot be compromised. Let me make this abundantly clear.

These are not conceived grandiose. My message to you is not one of an ominous apocalyptic doomsayer.

God has revealed to us through his prophets of those things to come. The Lord, however, has the power to con- trol and direct even the very thoughts of whomever he will, even in one's sleep. As he did in the days of old, he can still do it today!

God revealed to Daniel and the prophets many thousands of years ago the things that must surely come to pass, and Daniel did not understand all of the things he was shown. How much less you and I will be able to understand all things.

Perhaps there might be someone who, after reading my testimony, may be inspired by some words of comfort in knowing that a loving and a merciful God is able to save you anytime, anywhere, anyhow. All you have to do is to confess your sins to Jesus by asking Christ to forgive you of your sins and have mercy on your soul.

"A broken and a contrite heart, he will not despise." So said the Psalmist! "The sacrifices of God are a broken spirit: a broken and a contrite heart, O God, thou wilt not despise" (Ps. 51:17).

Allow me to use this sobering scenario at this time. Just think of a situation you might find yourself in, at any given time, where the possibility of death seems to be imminent. For example, imagine yourself being in an airplane disaster, of which we hear so much of in the news these days, or on a large or small boat, etc.

Case in point, let's think of a reallife situation, such as the horrific disaster of the famous luxury liner ship *Titanic*.

We are told that the song "Nearer, My God, to Thee" was the song of penitence the ship's chaplain chose to sing during their final moments of life when death was imminent. How convenient?

Ironically, those are some of the situations you may find yourself in, God forbid. Would you be able to say then it is well with your soul? Or can you now say it is well with your soul? If your answer is no, then why not ask Jesus to make it possible for you? No matter what the situation is in your life, Jesus is the answer.

Don't wait until you are immobilized or lying in your sickbed before you invite Jesus into your life. Even then, however, Christ is still willing and able to forgive you of your sins.

Why wait until then? Don't take such chances with your precious soul. Play it safe by insuring your soul with Christ today.

Right at this moment, he is at your door knocking. If you hear his voice, open up your heart and let him in!

He has the best insurance policy for your body and soul!

Death is a subject most people do not like to talk about. Ironically, in their moment of passion, they would make a statement in this manner, saying, "To die in a blaze of glory is the way they would like to go!"

Whether they are engaging in a fantasy of dying like a gladiator in an arena—a stunt person walking on a high wire to name just a few reasons—unlike those of a saint, however, some fantasies are deliberately premeditated and actually carried out as described in the above statements. But unfortunately, those people will never realize the blessings and glorious transformation of the death of a saint in the sight of the Lord.

The Bible said, "Precious in the sight of the Lord is the death of his saints" (Ps. 116:15).

I have purpose in my heart that if I should live a few more years, before I pass away from this life, I would like to live and die the death of a saint—praising and glorify- ing God.

Is there a better way to live and die? I don't think so!

10

THE PERFECT BLOOD TRANSFUSION THAT IS SAFE

Acquired Immunodeficiency Syndrome (AIDS)

Disease caused by strains of a virus, known as HIV (human immunodeficiency virus), that attacks cer tain white blood cells called T4 or CD4. According to medical science, the virus is spread through the exchange of body fluids (primarily semen, blood, and blood prod- ucts) and can persist in the body for a decade or more without any apparent symptoms.

Azidothymidine (AZT)

Drug used to treat patients infected with the human immunodeficiency virus (HIV), which cause AIDS, inhibits the virus's ability to reproduce and may decrease the frequency of infection by other diseases, enhancing the lives of HIV infected patients, but it does not cure AIDS.

Two other drugs that act similar to AZT, ddI (didanosine or dideoxyinosine) and da4 (stavadine), are used to treat patients who do not respond to or cannot tolerate AZT. Another similar acting drug, ddI (zalcit- abine or dideoxycytidine), is given in combination with AZT.

The disease weakens the body's immune system, allowing other diseases—including Kaposi sarcoma (a relatively uncommon and benign form of cancer), Pneumocystis carinii pneumonia, pulmonary tuberculosis, invasive cervical cancer, and encephalitis—to over- whelm the individual.

Very frightening! This is scary stuff. Nevertheless, there is hope that transcends all that scary stuff. Would you like to hear about it?

To whom it may concern: Allow me to recommend you to the best cure for the AIDS virus and all that ails you! In all fairness and honesty, however, the solution to your problems is the perfect blood transfusion that is safe from the AIDS virus: the blood atonement.

Divine Atonement

This divine atonement can be traced right back to the Garden of Eden when Adam and Eve's sins had separated them from their Creator, who, after He has created man in His own image and breathe into him the breath of life, man became a living soul, with body and spirit. Because of sin and disobedience, however, henceforth, the only thing that could atone and redeem man back to God his Creator is blood sacrifice of divine acceptance.

Further evidence of this fact has been demonstrated when the blood sacrifice of Abel, Adam's first son, was accepted unto God, but the sacrifice of Cain was rejected because it was not a blood sacrifice unto God his Creator!

God continues to demonstrate His love towards us, nevertheless, Jehovahjireh, through Christ our redeemer having being made the sacrificial Lamb. "The only begot- ten of the Father, full of grace and truth" (John 1:14). "The Lamb slain from the foundation of the world" (Rev. 13:8). "The blood of sprinkling, that speaketh bet- ter things than that of Abel" (Heb. 12:24) has shed his precious blood on the cross for our sins so that men and women of Adam's fallen race can be redeemed back into His favor, again.

Oh, what marvelous plan and act of redeeming love the Father has demonstrated to redeem the fallen man. Only Jehovahjireh, our Creator and provider, can deliver after this sort! Not an inanimate fossil rock or mere mortal with finite limitations.

Is there any other who is like the omnipotent, omni- scient, all-knowing God who could have made man from the dust of the ground into a living being having a soul, body, and spirit?

There is no other God who can deliver after this sort. No sculptured work of art and science based on the theory of evolution can create flesh and blood out of the dust of the ground like God the Creator has done!

Let us continue with the discussion of the unique, life-given power of blood atonement! Has there ever been? On the other hand, will there ever be a mere mortal? Whither by means of cloning or artificial insemination, who will ever produce a near-perfect species in the form of a human being? Then breathe the breath of life into what he has made as flesh and blood. The answer to the question is a resounding *no*!

Let the Word of God stand sure, that is, with God, there is no equal. Neither is there any likeness unto Him.

Therefore, any attempt made to imitate or duplicate any act of God's creation, one would have to be able to make something out of nothing.

However, only the true and living God can create something out of nothing. There you have the absolute fact of the authentic proof of creation. By this may all men know! Only the perfect blood of the Lamb of God can truly atone for the sins of man, whom He has created, and that is the fact that wins every contest!

Food for Thought for the Inquiring Mind

Here is some "food for thought" for all concerned: we are living in a very fearful time in history where everyone is afraid of the dreaded disease called AIDS.

It has been said AIDS is transmitted through body fluids (primarily semen, blood, and contaminated blood products) through the bloodstream of the body. To the layperson not extensively trained in the physiology of the human body, one might ask why through the blood stream. This is what the Bible has to say about it! We read in Leviticus 17:11 to the following: "For the life of the flesh is in the blood, and I have given it to you upon the altar to make atonement for your souls, for it is the blood that maketh atonement for the soul."

That is right, the life is in the blood, therefore if the blood is contaminated, it will eventually destroy the whole body.

For the said reasons, who therefore in his or her right mind would want to mingle with contaminated blood? Think of one person in this world who is dearest to you. No doubt the majority of people would say their mother or their wife or whomever he or she may be. Because of the fear of AIDS in the world today, no one wants to be given a questionable transfusion or one mingled with con- taminated blood. Not even if you were aware that that contaminated blood is the blood of your dearest love one.

There is one person whose blood not only mingles with my blood, whose blood I am not afraid of catching AIDS from because it has washed me, cleansed me, and made me whole! That precious blood is none other than that of our Lord Jesus Christ.

May I say this, however, in order to save us from the impending judgment of God, let us make sure we are washed with the blood that can save us and not destroy us with the AIDS virus, and the ultimate destruction that follows, which is death and hell. According to Romans 5:9, "Much more then, being now justified by his blood, we shall be saved from wrath through him."

In Ephesians 1:7, we read, "In whom we have redemption through his blood, the forgiveness of sins, according to the riches of his grace."

The blood of Jesus is perfect, in grace and mercy, for the atonement of sin; the apostle Paul reiterates the same proclamation concerning the redemptive power of the blood of Jesus as declared above.

Now found in Colossians 1:14, that reads likewise, "In whom we have redemption through his blood, even the forgiveness of sins,"

In summation of this subject concerning the blood of Jesus and its redemptive power to forgive sins, let us now focus on the need for confessing our sins to Jesus. The effectiveness of his cleansing blood that atones for our sins, according to 1 John 1:7–10, reads, "But if we walk in the light, as he is in the light, we have fellowship one with another, and the blood of Jesus Christ his Son cleanseth us from all sin. If we say that we have no sin, we deceive ourselves, and the truth is not in us. If we confess our sins, he is faithful and just to forgive us of all sins, and to cleanse us from all unrighteousness. If we say that we have not sinned, we make him a liar, and his word is not in us." Praise the Lord!

There you have it! The infallible word of truth, proclaiming the blood of Jesus to be the only blood that can save souls! There is no fear in this blood. The only fear is found in those who refused to accept its cleansing power to forgive sins.

A Soul Is a Precious Thing to Waste!

As I come to the closing chapter of my testimony, I am closing with these thoughts: For without faith, it is impossible to please God for he that cometh to God must believe that he is, and that he is a rewarder of them that diligently seek him (Heb. 11:6). By faith the harlot Rahab perished not with them that believed not, when she had received the spies with peace (Heb. 11:31). And what shall I more say?

For the time would fail me to tell of Gedeon, and of Barrak, and of Samson, and of Jephthah, of David also, and of Samuel, and of the prophets—who through faith subdued kingdoms, wrought righteousness, obtained promises, stopped the mouths of lions, quenched the violence of fire, escaped the edge of the sword, out of weakness were made strong, waxed valiant in flight, and turned to flight the armies of the aliens. Women received their dead raised to life again, and others were tortured, not accepting deliverance, that they might obtain a better resurrection. And others had trial of cruel mocking and scourging, yea, moreover of bonds and imprisonment.

They were stoned, they were torn asunder, were tempted, were slain with the sword. They wandered about in sheep- skins and goatskins being destitute, afflicted, tormented (of whom the world was not worthy). They wandered in deserts and in mountains and in dens and caves of the earth.

And these all, having obtained a good report through faith, received not the promise, "God having provided some better thing for us, that they without us should not be made perfect" (Heb. 11:40). You may read verses 1–40 for the complete amazing examples of faith.

As God has given each of us a measure of faith, let us all especially those of the household of faith who lead an exemplary life of faith as these heroic men and women of God.

"Finally, my brethren, be strong in the Lord and in the power of his might….Stand, therefore, having your loins girt about with truth, and having on the breastplate of righteousness; And your feet shod with the preparation of the gospel of peace; Above all, taking the shield of faith, wherewith ye shall be able to quench all the fiery darts of the wicked. And take the helmet of salvation, and the sword of the Spirit, which is the word of God" (Eph. 6:10, 14–17).

Conclusion

In my conclusion: I ever, state positively; declare with confidence! There is only one way to Heaven, which is the straight and narrow; unlike the polyglot communi- ties and bifurcated paths to New York City; affirmed by the Author and finisher of truth, declared in John 14: 6; Matthew 7: 13,14

Jesus said unto him; I am the way, the truth, and the life: no man cometh unto the Father, but by me.

I conclude with these words of a declaration by the Omniscient, Omnipresence, Omnipotent, (Maker of Heaven and Earth), at whose feet, every knee shall bow, and every tongue shall confess: "As I live, saith the Lord, every knee shall bow to me, and every tongue shall confess to God." Roman 14: 11. I hope you found this book for the inquiring mind, an insightful and engaging read. Read more: www.simeonwjohnson.com and Amazon & Barnes & Noble.com

For more information about my other books,

ROMW vs. RAMB Reveals God, Adam, and Creation
You're a Worthwhile Person in More Ways than a Million
Unforgettable Tribute to Our Heroes and Victims of 9/11

Visit www.simeonwjohnson.com

www.ingramcontent.com/pod-product-compliance
Lightning Source LLC
Chambersburg PA
CBHW021429070526
44577CB00001B/137